2ND EDITION

Birds *of the* Dakotas

Field Guide

T0160270

Stan Tekiela

Adventure Publications
Cambridge, Minnesota

Edited by Sandy Livoti and Dan Downing

Cover, book design and illustrations by Jonathan Norberg

Range maps produced by Anthony Hertzel

Cover photo: Baltimore Oriole by Stan Tekiela; background by Gestalt Imagery/Shutterstock
All photos by Stan Tekiela except p. 258 (main) by **Agami Photo Agency/Shutterstock**; p. 328 (non-breeding male) by **Paul Bannick**; pp. 52 (non-breeding male), 114, 304 (juvenile) and 328 (female) by **Rick and Nora Bowers**; p. 180 (displaying) by **Dudley Edmondson**; p. 54 (breeding male) by **Kevin T. Karlson**; p. 124 (female) by **Brian E. Small**; pp. 44 (juvenile), 160 (both juveniles), 208 (intermediate morph & both dark morphs), 214 (juvenile perching), 264 (juvenile), and 266 (in-flight juvenile) by **Brian K. Wheeler**; and pp. 38 (main), 206 (female), 262 (main), and 318 (female) by **Jim Zipp**

10 9 8 7 6 5 4 3 2 1
Birds of the Dakotas Field Guide
First Edition 2003
Second Edition 2022
Copyright © 2003 and 2022 by Stan Tekiela
Published by Adventure Publications
An imprint of AdventureKEEN
310 Garfield Street South
Cambridge, Minnesota 55008
(800) 678-7006
www.adventurepublications.net
All rights reserved
Printed in the United States of America
ISBN 978-1-64755-192-6 (pbk.); ISBN 978-1-64755-193-3 (ebook)

Birds that are mostly black p. 25

Birds that are mostly black and white p. 49

Birds that are mostly blue p. 83

Birds that are mostly brown p. 99

Birds that are mostly gray p. 227

Birds that have prominent green p. 279

Birds that have prominent orange p. 287

Birds that have prominent red p. 293

Birds that are mostly white p. 303

Birds that have prominent yellow p. 317

TABLE OF CONTENTS

Introduction
What's New? 6
Why Watch Birds in the Dakotas? 7
Observe with a Strategy: Tips for Identifying Birds. 8
Bird Basics 11
Bird Color Variables 11
Bird Nests. 13
Who Builds the Nest? 16
Fledging. 16
Why Birds Migrate 16
How Do Birds Migrate? 18
How to Use This Guide 20
Range Maps. 21

Sample Pages 22–23

The Birds
Black 25
Black and White 49
Blue 83
Brown 99
Gray 227
Green 279
Orange 287
Red 293
White 303
Yellow 317

Birding on the Internet 334
Checklist/Index by Species 335
More for the Dakotas 338
About the Author 340

WHAT'S NEW?

It is hard to believe that it's been more than 15 years since the debut of *Birds of the Dakotas Field Guide*. This critically acclaimed field guide has helped countless people identify and enjoy the birds that we love. Now, in this expanded second edition, *Birds of the Dakotas Field Guide* has many new and exciting changes and a fresh look, while retaining the same familiar, easy-to-use format.

To help you identify even more birds in the Dakotas, I have added 8 new species and more than 150 new color photographs. All of the range maps have been meticulously reviewed, and many updates have been made to reflect the ever-changing movements of the birds.

Everyone's favorite section, "Stan's Notes," has been expanded to include even more natural history information. "Compare" sections have been updated to help ensure that you correctly identify your bird, and additional feeder information has been added to help with bird feeding. I hope you will enjoy this great new edition as you continue to learn about and appreciate our North and South Dakota birds!

WHY WATCH BIRDS IN THE DAKOTAS?

Millions of people have discovered bird feeding. It's a simple and enjoyable way to bring the beauty of birds closer to your home. Watching birds at your feeder often leads to a lifetime pursuit of bird identification. The *Birds of the Dakotas Field Guide* is for those who want to identify common birds of North Dakota and South Dakota.

There are over 1,100 species of birds found in North America. In North and South Dakota there have been more than 400 different kinds of birds recorded through the years. These bird sightings were diligently recorded by hundreds of bird watchers and became part of the official state record. From these valuable records, I've chosen 133 of the most common birds of North and South Dakota to include in this field guide.

Bird watching, or birding, is one of the most popular activities in America. Its outstanding appeal in the Dakotas is due, in part, to an unusually rich and abundant birdlife. Why are there so many birds? One reason is open space. North Dakota is over 70,700 square miles (183,800 sq. km) and is the eighteenth-largest state. South Dakota is even larger, covering more than 77,100 square miles (200,400 sq. km), and is the seventeenth-largest state. Combined, these states make up a large portion of the North Central region and provide the majority of nesting habitats for a large number of birds, especially waterfowl, in this area of the U.S.

Vast open spaces in the Dakotas are not the only reason there is such an abundance of birds. It's also the diversity of habitat. The Dakotas can be broken into two distinct regions, each of which supports a different group of birds.

The highest and driest part of the Dakotas is in the western half. Called the Great Plains, this region has major features that are quite unlike its wide-open plains. The Black Hills and

Badlands are highly unique jewels and wonderful places to see birds such as Western Tanagers and Lazuli Buntings. The rest of the region is a relatively flat, open space that was once short grass prairie, but is now mostly agricultural. Horned Larks, Lark Buntings, Western Kingbirds and many other open-country birds can be found here.

The eastern half of the Dakotas is exemplified by the wide, flat, former lake bottom known as Glacial Lake Agassiz. This region, with its many temporary ponds and lakes, is much wetter than its western counterpart. These habitats provide very important breeding grounds for waterfowl such as Gadwalls and Mallards.

Not only do the Dakotas have varying habitats, there are variations in the weather. Since the two states extend over 450 miles (725 km) from north to south, the weather ranges greatly. While summers can be extremely hot and steamy, the high winds and driving snows of winter are legendary.

No matter where you are in the Dakotas there are birds to watch in every season. Whether witnessing a migration of millions of waterfowl in autumn or welcoming back shorebirds in spring, there is variety and excitement in birding as each season turns to the next.

OBSERVE WITH A STRATEGY: TIPS FOR IDENTIFYING BIRDS

Identifying birds isn't as difficult as you might think. By simply following a few basic strategies, you can increase your chances of successfully identifying most birds that you see. One of the first and easiest things to do when you see a new bird is to note **its color.** This field guide is organized by color, so simply turn to the right color section to find it.

Next, note the **size of the bird.** A strategy to quickly estimate size is to compare different birds. Pick a small, a medium and a large bird. Select an American Robin as the medium bird. Measured from bill tip to tail tip, a robin is 10 inches (25 cm). Now select two other birds, one smaller and one larger. Good choices are a House Sparrow, at about 6 inches (15 cm), and an American Crow, around 18 inches (45 cm). When you see a species you don't know, you can now quickly ask yourself, "Is it larger than a sparrow but smaller than a robin?" When you look in your field guide to identify your bird, you would check the species that are roughly 6–10 inches (15–25 cm). This will help to narrow your choices.

Next, note the **size, shape and color of the bill.** Is it long or short, thick or thin, pointed or blunt, curved or straight? Seed-eating birds, such as Northern Cardinals, have bills that are thick and strong enough to crack even the toughest seeds. Birds that sip nectar, such as Ruby-throated Hummingbirds, need long, thin bills to reach deep into flowers. Hawks and owls tear their prey with very sharp, curving bills. Sometimes, just noting the bill shape can help you decide whether the bird is a woodpecker, finch, grosbeak, blackbird or bird of prey.

Next, take a look around and note the **habitat** in which you see the bird. Is it wading in a saltwater marsh? Walking along a riverbank or on the beach? Soaring in the sky? Is it perched high in the trees or hopping along the forest floor? Because of diet and habitat preferences, you'll often see robins hopping on the ground but not usually eating seeds at a feeder. Or you'll see a Blue Jay sitting on a tree branch but not climbing headfirst down the trunk, like a Red-breasted Nuthatch would.

Noticing **what the bird is eating** will give you another clue to help you identify the species. Feeding is a big part of any bird's life. Fully one-third of all bird activity revolves around searching for food, catching prey and eating. While birds don't always follow all the rules of their diet, you can make some general assumptions. Northern Flickers, for instance, feed on ants and other insects, so you wouldn't expect to see them visiting a seed feeder. Other birds, such as Barn and Cliff Swallows, eat flying insects and spend hours swooping and diving to catch a meal.

Sometimes you can identify a bird by **the way it perches.** Body posture can help you differentiate between an American Crow and a Red-tailed Hawk, for example. Crows lean forward over their feet on a branch, while hawks perch in a vertical position. Consider posture the next time you see an unidentified large bird in a tree.

Birds in flight are harder to identify, but noting the **wing size and shape** will help. Wing size is in direct proportion to body size, weight and type of flight. Wing shape determines whether the bird flies fast and with precision, or slowly and less precisely. Barn Swallows, for instance, have short, pointed wings that slice through the air, enabling swift, accurate flight. Turkey Vultures have long, broad wings for soaring on warm updrafts. House Finches have short, rounded wings, helping them to flit through thick tangles of branches.

Some bird species have a unique **pattern of flight** that can help in identification. American Goldfinches fly in a distinctive undulating pattern that makes it look like they're riding a roller coaster.

While it's not easy to make all of these observations in the short time you often have to watch a "mystery" bird, practicing these identification methods will greatly expand your birding skills. To further improve your skills, seek the guidance of a more experienced birder who can answer your questions on the spot.

BIRD BASICS

It's easier to identify birds and communicate about them if you know the names of the different parts of a bird. For instance, it's more effective to use the word "crest" to indicate the set of extra-long feathers on top of a Northern Cardinal's head than to try to describe it.

The following illustration points out the basic parts of a bird. Because it is a composite of many birds, it shouldn't be confused with any actual bird.

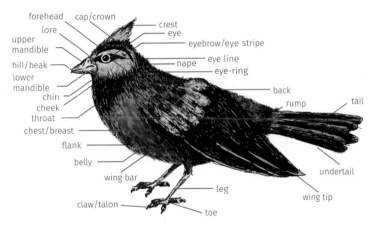

Bird Color Variables

No other animal has a color palette like a bird's. Brilliant blues, lemon yellows, showy reds and iridescent greens are common in the bird world. In general, male birds are more colorful than their female counterparts. This helps males attract a mate, essentially saying, "Hey, look at me!" Color calls attention to a male's health as well. The better the condition of his feathers, the better his food source, territory and potential for mating.

Male and female birds that don't look like each other are called sexually dimorphic, meaning "two forms." Dimorphic females often have a nondescript dull color, as seen in Lazuli Buntings. Muted tones help females hide during the weeks of motionless incubation and draw less attention to them when they're out feeding or taking a break from the rigors of raising the young.

The males of some species, such as the Downy Woodpecker, Blue Jay and Bald Eagle, look nearly identical to the females. In woodpeckers, the sexes are differentiated by only a red mark, or sometimes a yellow mark. Depending on the species, the mark may be on top of the head, on the face or nape of neck, or just behind the bill.

During the first year, juvenile birds often look like their mothers. Since brightly colored feathers are used mainly for attracting a mate, young non-breeding males don't have a need for colorful plumage. It's not until the first spring molt (or several years later, depending on the species) that young males obtain their breeding colors.

Both breeding and winter plumages are the result of molting. Molting is the process of dropping old, worn feathers and replacing them with new ones. All birds molt, typically twice a year, with the spring molt usually occurring in late winter. At this time, most birds produce their brighter breeding plumage, which lasts throughout the summer.

Winter plumage is the result of the late summer molt, which serves a couple of important functions. First, it adds feathers for warmth in the coming winter season. Second, in some species it produces feathers that tend to be drab in color, which helps to camouflage the birds and hide them from predators. The winter plumage of the male American Goldfinch, for example, is olive-brown, unlike its canary-yellow breeding color during summer. Luckily for us, some birds, such as the male Northern Cardinal, retain their bright summer colors all year long.

Bird Nests

Bird nests are a true feat of engineering. Imagine constructing a home that's strong enough to weather storms, large enough to hold your entire family, insulated enough to shelter them from cold and heat, and waterproof enough to keep out rain. Think about building it without blueprints or directions and using mainly your feet. Birds do this!

Before building, birds must select an appropriate site. In some species, such as the House Wren, the male picks out several potential sites and assembles small twigs in each. The "extra" nests, called dummy nests, discourage other birds from using any nearby cavities for their nests. The male takes the female around and shows her the choices. After choosing her favorite, she finishes the construction.

In other species, such as the Baltimore Oriole, the female selects the site and builds the nest, while the male offers an occasional suggestion. Each bird species has its own nest-building routine that is strictly followed.

As you can see in these illustrations, birds build a wide variety of nest types.

ground nest   **platform nest**   **cup nest**   **pendulous nest**   **cavity nest**

Nesting material often consists of natural items found in the immediate area. Most nests consist of plant fibers (such as bark from grapevines), sticks, mud, dried grass, feathers, fur, or soft, fuzzy tufts from thistle. Some birds, including Ruby-throated Hummingbirds, use spiderwebs to glue nest materials together.

Transportation of nesting material is limited to the amount a bird can hold or carry. Birds must make many trips afield to gather enough material to complete a nest. Most nests take four days or more, and hundreds, if not thousands, of trips to build.

A **ground nest** can be a mound of vegetation on the ground or in the water. It can also be just a simple, shallow depression scraped out in earth, stones or sand. Killdeer and Horned Larks scrape out ground nests without adding any nesting material.

The **platform nest** represents a much more complex type of construction. Typically built with twigs or sticks and branches, this nest forms a platform and has a depression in the center to nestle the eggs. Platform nests can be in trees; on balconies, cliffs, bridges, or man-made platforms; and even in flowerpots. They often provide space for the adventurous young and function as a landing platform for the parents.

Mourning Doves and herons don't anchor their platform nests to trees, so these can tumble from branches during high winds and storms. Hawks, eagles, ospreys and other birds construct sturdier platform nests with large sticks and branches.

Other platform nests are constructed on the ground with mud, grass and other vegetation from the area. Many waterfowl build platform nests on the ground near or in water. A **floating platform nest** moves with the water level, preventing the nest, eggs and birds from being flooded.

Three-quarters of all songbirds construct a **cup nest,** which is a modified platform nest. The supporting platform is built first and attached firmly to a tree, shrub, or rock ledge or the ground. Next, the sides are constructed with grass, small twigs, bark or leaves, which are woven together and often glued with mud for added strength. The inner cup can be lined with down feathers, animal fur or hair, or soft plant materials and is contoured last.

The **pendulous nest** is an unusual nest that looks like a sock hanging from a branch. Attached to the end of small branches of trees, this unique nest is inaccessible to most predators and often waves wildly in a breeze.

Woven tightly with plant fibers, the pendulous nest is strong and watertight and takes up to a week to build. A small opening at the top or on the side allows parents access to the grass-lined interior. More commonly used by tropical birds, this complex nest has also been mastered by orioles and kinglets. It must be one heck of a ride to be inside one of these nests during a windy spring thunderstorm!

The **cavity nest** is used by many species of birds, most notably woodpeckers and Eastern Bluebirds. A cavity nest is often excavated from a branch or tree trunk and offers shelter from storms, sun, cold and predators. A small entrance hole in a tree can lead to a nest chamber that is up to a safe 10 inches (25 cm) deep.

Typically made by woodpeckers, cavity nests are usually used only once by the builder. Nest cavities can be used for many subsequent years by such inhabitants as Wood Ducks, Tree Swallows and bluebirds. Kingfishers, on the other hand, can dig a tunnel up to 4 feet (about 1 m) long in a riverbank. The nest chamber at the end of the tunnel is already well insulated, so it's usually only sparsely lined.

One of the most clever of all nests is the **no nest,** or daycare nest. Parasitic birds, such as Brown-headed Cowbirds, don't build their own nests. Instead, the egg-laden female searches out the nest of another bird and sneaks in to lay an egg while the host mother isn't looking.

A mother cowbird wastes no energy building a nest only to have it raided by a predator. Laying her eggs in the nests of other birds transfers the responsibility of raising her young to the host. When she lays her eggs in several nests, the chances increase that at least one of her babies will live to maturity.

Who Builds the Nest?

Generally, the female bird constructs the nest. She gathers the materials and does the building, with an occasional visit from her mate to check on progress. In some species, both parents contribute equally to nest building. The male may forage for sticks, grass or mud, but it is the female that often fashions the nest. Only rarely does a male build a nest by himself.

Fledging

Fledging is the time between hatching and flight, or leaving the nest. Some species of birds are **precocial,** meaning they leave the nest within hours of hatching, though it may be weeks before they can fly. This is common in waterfowl and shorebirds.

Baby birds that hatch naked and blind need to stay in the nest for a few weeks (these birds are **altricial**). Baby birds that are still in the nest are **nestlings.** Until birds start to fly, they are called **fledglings.**

Why Birds Migrate

Why do so many species of birds migrate? The short answer is simple: food. Birds migrate to locations with abundant food, as it is easier to breed where there is food than where food is scarce. Western Tanagers, for instance, are **complete migrators** that fly from the tropics of South America to nest in the forests of North America, where billions of newly hatched insects are available to feed to their young.

Other migrators, such as some birds of prey, migrate back to northern regions in spring. In these locations, they hunt mice, voles and other small rodents that are beginning to breed.

Complete migrators have a set time and pattern of migration. Every year at nearly the same time, they head to a specific wintering ground. Complete migrators may travel great distances, sometimes 15,000 miles (24,100 km) or more in one year.

Complete migration doesn't necessarily imply flying from the cold, frozen northland to a tropical destination. The Dark-eyed Junco, for example, is a complete migrator that flies from the far reaches of Canada to spend the winter right here in the Dakotas. This trip is still considered complete migration.

Complete migrators have many interesting aspects. In spring, males often leave a few weeks before the females, arriving early to scope out possibilities for nesting sites and food sources, and to begin to defend territories. The females arrive several weeks later. In many species, the females and their young leave earlier in the fall, often up to four weeks before the adult males.

Other species, such as the American Goldfinch, are **partial migrators**. These birds usually wait until their food supplies dwindle before flying south. Unlike complete migrators, partial migrators move only far enough south, or sometimes east and west, to find abundant food. In some years it might be only a few hundred miles, while in other years it can be as much as a thousand. This kind of migration, dependent on weather and the availability of food, is sometimes called seasonal movement.

Unlike the predictable complete migrators or partial migrators, **irruptive migrators** can move every third to fifth year or, in some cases, in consecutive years. These migrations are triggered when times are tough and food is scarce. Red-breasted Nuthatches are irruptive migrators. They leave their normal northern range in search of more food or in response to overpopulation.

Many other birds don't migrate at all. Black-capped Chickadees, for example, are **non-migrators** that remain in their habitat all year long and just move around as necessary to find food.

How Do Birds Migrate?

One of the many secrets of migration is fat. While most people are fighting the ongoing battle of the bulge, birds intentionally gorge themselves to gain as much fat as possible without losing the ability to fly. Fat provides the greatest amount of energy per unit of weight. In the same way that your car needs gas, birds are propelled by fat and stall without it.

During long migratory flights, fat deposits are used up quickly, and birds need to stop to refuel. This is when backyard bird feeding stations and undeveloped, natural spaces around our towns and cities are especially important. Some birds require up to 2–3 days of constant feeding to build their fat reserves before continuing their seasonal trip.

Many birds, such as most eagles, hawks, ospreys, falcons and vultures, migrate during the day. Larger birds can hold more body fat, go longer without eating and take longer to migrate. These birds glide along on rising columns of warm air, called thermals, that hold them aloft while they slowly make their way north or south. They generally rest at night and hunt early in the morning before the sun has a chance to warm the land and create good soaring conditions. Daytime migrators use a combination of landforms, rivers, and the rising and setting sun to guide them in the right direction.

The majority of small birds, called **passerines,** migrate at night. Studies show that some use the stars to navigate. Others use the setting sun, and still others, such as doves, use Earth's magnetic field to guide them north or south.

While flying at night may not seem like a good idea, it's actually safer. First, there are fewer avian predators hunting for birds at night. Second, night travel allows time during the day to find food in unfamiliar surroundings. Third, wind patterns at night tend to be flat, or laminar. Flat winds don't have the turbulence of daytime winds and can help push the smaller birds along.

HOW TO USE THIS GUIDE

To help you quickly and easily identify birds, this field guide is organized by color. Refer to the color key on the first page, note the color of the bird, and turn to that section. For example, the male Rose-breasted Grosbeak is black and white with a red patch on its chest. Because the bird is mostly black-and-white, it will be found in the black-and-white section.

Each color section is also arranged by size, generally with the smaller birds first. Sections may also incorporate the average size in a range, which in some cases reflects size differences between male and female birds. Flip through the pages in the color section to find the bird. If you already know the name of the bird, check the index for the page number.

In some species, the male and female are very different in color. In others, the breeding and winter plumage colors differ. These species will have an inset photograph with a page reference and will be found in two color sections.

You will find a variety of information in the bird description sections. To learn more, turn to the sample on pp. 22–23.

Range Maps

Range maps are included for each bird. Colored areas indicate where the bird is frequently found. The colors represent the presence of a species during a specific season, not the density, or amount, of birds in the area. Green is used for summer, blue for winter, red for year-round and yellow for migration.

While every effort has been made to depict accurate ranges, these are constantly in flux due to a variety of factors. Changing weather, habitat, species abundance and availability of vital resources, such as food and water, can affect the migration and movement of local populations, causing birds to be found in areas that are atypical for the species. So please use the maps as intended—as general guides only.

female
p. 327

male

Common Name

Range Map   *Scientific name*   Color Indicator

YEAR-ROUND
SUMMER
MIGRATION
WINTER

Size: measurement is from head to tip of tail; wingspan may be listed as well

Male: brief description of the male bird; may include breeding, winter or other plumages

Female: brief description of the female bird, which is sometimes different from the male

Juvenile: brief description of the juvenile bird, which often looks like the adult female

Nest: kind of nest the bird builds to raise its young; who builds it; number of broods per year

Eggs: number of eggs you might expect to see in a nest; color and marking

Incubation: average days the parents spend incubating the eggs; who does the incubation

Fledging: average days the young spend in the nest after hatching but before they leave the nest; who does the most "childcare" and feeding

Migration: type of migrator: complete (seasonal, consistent), partial (seasonal, destination varies), irruptive (unpredictable, depends on the food supply) or non-migrator

Food: what the bird eats most of the time (e.g., seeds, insects, fruit, nectar, small mammals, fish) and whether it typically comes to a bird feeder

Compare: notes about other birds that look similar and the pages on which they can be found; may include extra information to aid in identification

Stan's Notes: Interesting natural history information. This could be something to look or listen for or something to help positively identify the bird. Also includes remarkable features.

female
p. 143

male

Brown-headed Cowbird
Molothrus ater

SUMMER

Size:	7½" (19 cm)
Male:	Glossy black with a chocolate-brown head. Dark eyes. Pointed, sharp gray bill.
Female:	dull brown with a pointed, sharp, gray bill
Juvenile:	similar to female but with dull-gray plumage and a streaked chest
Nest:	no nest; lays eggs in nests of other birds
Eggs:	5–7; white with brown markings
Incubation:	10–13 days; host birds incubate eggs
Fledging:	10–11 days; host birds feed the young
Migration:	complete, to southern states
Food:	insects, seeds; will come to seed feeders
Compare:	The male Red-winged Blackbird (p. 31) is slightly larger with red-and-yellow patches on upper wings. Common Grackle (p. 37) has a long tail and lacks the brown head. European Starling (p. 27) has a shorter tail.

Stan's Notes: Cowbirds are members of the blackbird family. Of approximately 750 species of parasitic birds worldwide, this is the only parasitic bird in the Dakotas. Brood parasites lay their eggs in the nests of other birds, leaving the host birds to raise their young. Cowbirds are known to have laid their eggs in the nests of over 200 species of birds. While some birds reject cowbird eggs, most incubate them and raise the young, even to the exclusion of their own. Look for warblers and other birds feeding young birds twice their own size. Named "Cowbird" for its habit of following bison and cattle herds to feed on insects flushed up by the animals.

winter

breeding

YEAR-ROUND

European Starling
Sturnus vulgaris

Size: 7½" (19 cm)

Male: Glittering, iridescent purplish black in spring and summer; duller and speckled with white in fall and winter. Long, pointed, yellow bill in spring; gray in fall. Pointed wings. Short tail.

Female: same as male

Juvenile: similar to adults, with grayish-brown plumage and a streaked chest

Nest: cavity; male and female line cavity; 2 broods per year

Eggs: 4–6; bluish with brown markings

Incubation: 12–14 days; female and male incubate

Fledging: 18–20 days; female and male feed the young

Migration: non-migrator to partial migrator; some will move to southern states

Food: insects, seeds, fruit; visits seed or suet feeders

Compare: The Common Grackle (p. 37) has a long tail. The male Brown-headed Cowbird (p. 25) has a brown head. Look for the shiny, dark feathers to help identify the European Starling.

Stan's Notes: One of our most numerous songbirds. Mimics the songs of up to 20 bird species and imitates sounds, including the human voice. Jaws are more powerful when opening than when closing, enabling the bird to pry open crevices to find insects. Often displaces woodpeckers, chickadees and other cavity-nesting birds. Large families gather with blackbirds in the fall. Not a native bird; 100 starlings were introduced to New York City in 1890–91 from Europe. Bill changes color in spring and fall.

female
p. 155

Spotted Towhee
Pipilo maculatus

SUMMER MIGRATION

Size: 8½" (22 cm)

Male: Mostly black with dirty red-brown sides and a white belly. Multiple white spots on wings and sides. Long black tail with a white tip. Rich, red eyes.

Female: very similar to male but with a brown head

Juvenile: brown with a heavily streaked chest

Nest: cup; female builds; 1–2 broods per year

Eggs: 3–5; white with brown markings

Incubation: 12–14 days; female and male incubate

Fledging: 10–12 days; female and male feed young

Migration: complete, to southern states

Food: seeds, fruit, insects

Compare: American Robin (p. 253) is larger. Male Rose-breasted Grosbeak (p. 57) has a rosy patch in center of chest.

Stan's Notes: Summer visitor in western and southern parts of the Dakotas and seen during migration. Found in a variety of habitats from thick brush and forest edges to suburban backyards. Usually heard noisily scratching through dead leaves on the ground for food. Over 70 percent of its diet is plant material. Eats more insects during spring and summer. Well known to retreat from danger by walking away rather than taking to flight. Nest is nearly always on the ground under bushes but away from where the male perches to sing. Song and plumage vary geographically and aren't well studied or understood.

female
p. 153

male

Red-winged Blackbird
Agelaius phoeniceus

YEAR-ROUND
SUMMER

Size: 8½" (22 cm)

Male: Jet black with red-and-yellow patches (epaulets) on upper wings. Pointed black bill.

Female: heavily streaked brown with a pointed brown bill and white eyebrows

Juvenile: same as female

Nest: cup; female builds; 2–3 broods per year

Eggs: 3–4; bluish green with brown markings

Incubation: 10–12 days; female incubates

Fledging: 11–14 days; female and male feed the young

Migration: complete to partial migrator, to southern states, Mexico and Central America; will move around to find food

Food: seeds, insects; visits seed and suet feeders

Compare: The male Brown-headed Cowbird (p. 25) is smaller and glossier and has a brown head. The bold red-and-yellow epaulets distinguish the male Red-winged from other blackbirds.

Stan's Notes: One of the most widespread and numerous birds in the Dakotas. Found around marshes, wetlands, lakes and rivers. Flocks with as many as 10,000 birds have been reported. Males arrive before the females and sing to defend their territory. The male repeats his call from the top of a cattail while showing off his red-and-yellow shoulder patches. The female chooses a mate and often builds her nest over shallow water in a thick stand of cattails. The male can be aggressive when defending the nest. Red-winged Blackbirds feed mostly on seeds in spring and fall, and insects throughout the summer.

in flight

Black Tern
Chlidonias niger

SUMMER
MIGRATION

Size: 9¾" (24.5 cm)

Male: Breeding plumage (March to September) head, neck and body are black. Back, wings and tail are gray. Dark eyes, bill and legs. Winter is overall gray with a nearly white head and white undertail. Pale-yellow legs.

Female: same as male

Juvenile: similar to winter adult, back is more brown than gray

Nest: floating platform; male and female build; 1–2 broods per year

Eggs: 2 4; green with brown markings

Incubation: 21–22 days; female and male incubate

Fledging: 21–28 days; male and female feed young

Migration: complete, to South America

Food: insects, small fish, aquatic insects

Compare: The only tern with a black head and body.

Stan's Notes: Common breeding bird in prairie potholes, nesting in small colonies. The nest is often just a floating mat of vegetation. Often will use an old grebe nest. Young females begin to breed at 2 years of age. Aggressively defends nest site and young. Will dive at intruders and predators. Has a unique buoyant flight pattern, with erratic swoops. Unlike other tern species, rarely plunges into water after prey. Hunts for insects on surfaces of ponds and marshes and picks insects out of the air. Occasionally follows plows to pick off insects disturbed in fields. Gives a sharp "keff" call while in flight. Migrates in large flocks.

female
p. 163

male

SUMMER

Yellow-headed Blackbird
Xanthocephalus xanthocephalus

Size: 9–11" (23–28 cm)

Male: Large black bird with a lemon-yellow head, breast and nape of neck. Black mask and gray bill. White wing patches.

Female: similar to male but slightly smaller with a brown body and dull-yellow head and chest

Juvenile: similar to female

Nest: cup; female builds; 2 broods per year

Eggs: 3–5; greenish white with brown markings

Incubation: 11–13 days; female incubates

Fledging: 9–12 days; female feeds the young

Migration: complete, to southern states and Mexico

Food: insects, seeds; will come to ground feeders

Compare: The male Red-winged Blackbird (p. 31) is smaller and has red-and-yellow patches on its wings. Look for the bright-yellow head to identify the male Yellow-headed.

Stan's Notes: Found around marshes, wetlands and lakes. Nests in deep water, unlike its cousin, the Red-winged Blackbird, which prefers shallow water. Usually heard before seen. Gives a raspy, low, metallic sounding call. The male is the only large black bird with a bright-yellow head. He gives an impressive mating display, flying with his head drooped and feet and tail pointing down while steadily beating his wings. Young keep low and out of sight for up to three weeks before they start to fly. Migrates in large flocks of as many as 200 birds, often with Red-winged Blackbirds and Brown-headed Cowbirds. Flocks of mainly males return in late March and early April; females return later. Most colonies consist of 20–100 nests.

Common Grackle
Quiscalus quiscula

Size:	11–13" (28–33 cm)
Male:	Large, iridescent blackbird with bluish-black head and purplish-brown body. Long black tail. Long, thin bill and bright-golden eyes.
Female:	similar to male but smaller and duller
Juvenile:	similar to female
Nest:	cup; female builds; 2 broods per year
Eggs:	4–5; greenish white with brown markings
Incubation:	13–14 days; female incubates
Fledging:	16–20 days; female and male feed the young
Migration:	complete migrator to partial, to southern states; will move around to find food
Food:	fruit, seeds, insects; will come to seed and suet feeders
Compare:	The European Starling (p. 27) is much smaller with a speckled appearance, and a yellow bill during breeding season. Male Red-winged Blackbird (p. 31) has red-and-yellow wing markings (epaulets).

Stan's Notes: Usually nests in small colonies of up to 75 pairs but travels with other blackbird species in large flocks. Known to feed in farm fields. The common name is derived from the Latin word *gracula*, meaning "jackdaw," another species of bird and a term that can refer to any bird in the *Quiscalus* genus. The male holds his tail in a deep V shape during flight. The flight pattern is usually level, as opposed to an undulating movement. Unlike most birds, it has larger muscles for opening its mouth than for closing it, enabling it to pry crevices apart to find hidden insects.

winter

Eared Grebe
Podiceps nigricollis

SUMMER

Size: 13" (33 cm)

Male: Breeding plumage (April to August) head, neck and back overall dark brown to black. Sides and chest are chestnut brown. Wispy yellow plumes feather out behind red eyes. Small black bill. Winter plumage chin and sides are dirty brown to black and white. Red eyes and a dark-tipped gray bill.

Female: same as male

Juvenile: similar to winter adult

Nest: floating platform; female and male build; 1–2 broods per year

Eggs: 3–5; light blue with brown markings

Incubation: 20–22 days; female and male incubate

Fledging: 20–40 days; male and female teach young what to eat

Migration: complete, to Pacific and Gulf coasts, Mexico

Food: fish, aquatic insects

Compare: Horned Grebe (p. 301) is slightly larger, with a rufous neck during breeding season.

Stan's Notes: A grebe of pothole lakes and ponds, nesting in large colonies. Builds a platform nest in shallow water, made from reeds and grasses. Often constructs more than one nest. A few days after hatching, the young are fed small feathers. Feather eating pads the stomach and is thought to aid the digestion of fish and fish bones. Chick siblings are not the same size, since young hatch several days apart. Chicks ride on backs of parents. Often dives underwater to avoid danger, remaining submerged with just its bill above water.

American Coot
Fulica americana

SUMMER

Size: 13–16" (33–40 cm)

Male: Gray-to-black waterbird. Duck-like white bill with a dark band near the tip and a small red patch near the eyes. Small white patch near base of tail. Green legs and feet. Red eyes.

Female: same as male

Juvenile: much paler than adults, with a gray bill

Nest: floating platform; female and male construct; 1 brood per year

Eggs: 9–12; pinkish buff with brown markings

Incubation: 21-25 days; female and male incubate

Fledging: 49–52 days; female and male feed young

Migration: complete, to southern states, Mexico and Central America

Food: insects, aquatic plants

Compare: Smaller than most waterfowl, it is the only black, duck-like bird with a white bill.

Stan's Notes: Usually seen in large flocks on open water. Not a duck, as it has large lobed toes instead of webbed feet. An excellent diver and swimmer, bobbing its head as it swims. A favorite food of Bald Eagles. It is not often seen in flight, unless it's trying to escape from an eagle. To take off, it scrambles across the surface of the water, flapping its wings. Gives a unique series of creaks, groans and clicks. Anchors its floating platform nest to vegetation. Huge flocks with as many as 1,000 birds gather for migration. Migrates at night. The common name "Coot" comes from the Middle English word *coote*, which was used to describe various waterfowl. Also called Mud Hen.

in flight

American Crow
Corvus brachyrhynchos

YEAR-ROUND
SUMMER

Size:	18" (45 cm)
Male:	All-black bird with black bill, legs and feet. Can have a purple sheen in direct sunlight.
Female:	same as male
Juvenile:	same as adult
Nest:	platform; female builds; 1 brood per year
Eggs:	4–6; bluish to olive-green with brown marks
Incubation:	18 days; female incubates
Fledging:	28–35 days; female and male feed the young
Migration:	non-migrator to partial migrator
Food:	fruit, insects, mammals, fish, carrion; will come to seed and suet feeders
Compare:	Black-billed Magpie (p. 73) has a long tail and white belly. Similar to Common Raven (not shown), but has a smaller bill and lacks shaggy throat feathers. The Crow has a higher-pitched call than Raven's deep, low raspy call. Crow has a squared tail. Raven has a wedge-shaped tail, apparent in flight.

Stan's Notes: One of the most recognizable birds in the Dakotas, found in most habitats. Imitates other birds and human voices. One of the smartest of all birds and very social, often entertaining itself by provoking chases with other birds. Eats roadkill but is rarely hit by vehicles. Can live as long as 20 years. Often reuses its nest every year if it's not taken over by a Great Horned Owl. Unmated birds, known as helpers, help to raise the young. Extended families roost together at night, dispersing daily to hunt. Cannot soar on thermals; flaps constantly and glides downward. Gathers in huge communal flocks of up to 10,000 birds in winter.

soaring

juvenile

drying

Turkey Vulture

Cathartes aura

SUMMER

Size: 26–32" (66–80 cm); up to 6' wingspan

Male: Large and black with a naked red head and legs. In flight, wings are two-toned with a black leading edge and a gray trailing edge. Wing tips end in finger-like projections. Tail is long and squared. Ivory bill.

Female: same as male but slightly smaller

Juvenile: similar to adults, with a gray-to-blackish head and bill

Nest: no nest or minimal nest, on a cliff or in a cave, sometimes in a hollow tree; 1 brood per year

Eggs: 1–3; white with brown markings

Incubation: 38–41 days; female and male incubate

Fledging: 66–88 days; female and male feed the young

Migration: complete, to southern states, Mexico and Central and South America

Food: carrion; parents regurgitate to feed the young

Compare: Bald Eagle (p. 81) is larger and lacks two-toned wings. Look for the obvious naked red head to identify the Turkey Vulture.

Stan's Notes: The naked head reduces the risk of feather fouling (picking up diseases) from contact with carcasses. It has a strong bill for tearing apart flesh. Unlike hawks and eagles, it has weak feet more suited for walking than grasping. One of the few birds with a developed sense of smell. Mostly mute, making only grunts and groans. Holds its wings in an upright V shape in flight. Teeters from wing tip to wing tip as it soars and hovers. Seen in trees with wings outstretched, sunning itself and drying after a rain.

in flight

juvenile

crests

drying

Double-crested Cormorant
Phalacrocorax auritus

Size: 31–35" (79–89 cm); up to 4⅓' wingspan

Male: Large black waterbird with unusual blue eyes and a long, snakelike neck. Large gray bill, with yellow at the base and a hooked tip.

Female: same as male

Juvenile: lighter brown with a grayish chest and neck

Nest: platform; male and female construct; 1 brood per year

Eggs: 3–4; bluish white without markings

Incubation: 25–29 days; female and male incubate

Fledging: 37–42 days; male and female feed the young

Migration: complete, to southern states, Mexico and Central America

Food: small fish, aquatic insects

Compare: The Turkey Vulture (p. 45) also spreads out its wings to dry in the sun, but it has a naked red head. The American Coot (p. 41) has a duck-like white bill. Look for the long, snakelike neck and large, hooked bill to help identify the Cormorant.

Stan's Notes: Flies in a large V or a line. Usually roosts in large colonies in trees close to water. Swims underwater to catch fish, holding its wings at its sides. This bird's outer feathers soak up water, but its body feathers don't. To dry off, it strikes an upright pose with wings outstretched, facing the sun. Gives grunts, pops and groans. Named "Double-crested" for the crests on its head, which are not often seen. "Cormorant" is a contraction from *corvus marinus*, meaning "crow" or "raven," and "of the sea."

male

female

Black-and-white Warbler

Mniotilta varia

Size: 5" (13 cm)

Male: Small with zebralike striping and a black-and-white striped crown. Black cheek patch and chin. White belly.

Female: duller than male and lacks a black cheek patch and chin

Juvenile: similar to female

Nest: cup; female builds; 1 brood per year

Eggs: 4–5; white with brown markings

Incubation: 10–11 days; female incubates

Fledging: 9–12 days; female and male feed the young

Migration: complete, to Florida, Mexico, and Central and South America

Food: insects

Compare: Climbs down tree trunks headfirst, like the White-breasted Nuthatch (p. 235) and Red-breasted Nuthatch (p. 229). Look for a small black-and-white bird climbing down trees to identify the Black-and-white Warbler.

Stan's Notes: This is the only warbler species that moves down tree trunks headfirst. Look for it searching for insect eggs in the bark of large trees. Its song sounds like a slowly turning, squeaky wheel going around and around. Female performs a distraction dance to draw predators away from the nest. Constructs its nest on the ground, concealing it under dead leaves or at the base of a tree. Found in a variety of habitats. Common summer resident that nests throughout the Dakotas. More conspicuous during migration. Most arrive in April and May and leave by September.

male

female

Downy Woodpecker
Dryobates pubescens

YEAR-ROUND

Size: 6½" (15 cm)

Male: Small woodpecker with a white belly and black-and-white spotted wings. Red mark on the back of the head and a white stripe down the back. Short black bill.

Female: same as male but lacks the red mark

Juvenile: same as female, some with a red mark near the forehead

Nest: cavity with a round entrance hole; male and female excavate; 1 brood per year

Eggs: 3–5; white without markings

Incubation: 11–12 days; female incubates during the day, male incubates at night

Fledging: 20–25 days; male and female feed the young

Migration: non-migrator

Food: insects, seeds; visits seed and suet feeders

Compare: The Hairy Woodpecker (p. 59) is larger. Look for the Downy's shorter, thinner bill.

Stan's Notes: This is one of the most abundant, widespread woodpeckers in the Dakotas, found throughout where tees are present. Stiff tail feathers help to brace it like a tripod as it clings to a tree. Like other woodpeckers, it has a long, barbed tongue to pull insects from tiny places. Mates drum on branches or hollow logs to announce territory, which is rarely larger than 5 acres (2 ha). Repeats a high-pitched "peek-peek" call. Male performs most of the brooding. During winter, it will roost in a cavity. Undulates in flight.

female
p. 129

breeding male

non-breeding male

Lark Bunting
Calamospiza melanocorys

Size: 6½" (16 cm)

Male: Short, stocky black bird with a large, broad head. White wing patches and large bluish-gray bill. Winter male is black, brown, gray and white-striped with white wing patches.

Female: overall brown with a heavily streaked chest, white belly, black vertical line on each side of white chin, may have a dark central spot on the chest, faint white eyebrows

Juvenile: similar to adult of the same sex

Nest: cup; female builds; 1–2 broods per year

Eggs: 4–6; pale blue with markings

Incubation: 11–13 days; female and male incubate

Fledging: 8–12 days; female and male feed young

Migration: complete, to southwestern states and Mexico

Food: insects, seeds

Compare: The breeding male's bold black-and-white plumage is hard to confuse with any other bird's. Look for the rather large broad head and large bill to help identify.

Stan's Notes: Common throughout, but is more abundant in the western third of the Dakotas in dry plains and sagebrush regions. Has short rounded wings. Has short rounded wings. Flying with shallow wingbeats, the male flashes white wing patches. Male takes to air to display to female, setting its wings in a V position and floating back, rocking like a butterfly, singing a most amazing song. Song is like the song of Old World larks, hence the common name. Will flock in fall with hundreds, if not thousands, of other Lark Buntings for migration.

breeding male

winter male

female

Snow Bunting
Plectrophenax nivalis

WINTER

Size: 7" (18 cm)

Male: Winter male has a white chin, breast and belly, and rusty brown head, back and shoulders. Small yellow bill. Black legs and feet. Breeding male is overall white with black-and-white wings.

Female: similar to breeding male, but lacks the all-white head

Juvenile: similar to winter male

Nest: cavity; female builds; 1–2 broods per year

Eggs: 4–7; green to blue with brown markings

Incubation: 10–16 days; female incubates

Fledging: 10–17 days; male and female feed young

Migration: complete to northern states

Food: insects, seeds

Compare: This bird is easy to identify since no other small sparrow-like bird has so much white.

Stan's Notes: A winter resident of the Dakotas. Often feeds on the ground along roads. Usually seen in flocks of up to 30 individuals of mixed ages and sexes. Individual Snow Buntings appear slightly different from each other; some are completely black and white, others are a combination of black, white, brown and rust. Winter plumage is seen from September to March. Sometimes seen with other winter birds such as Horned Larks and Lapland Longspurs. Female constructs a grass and moss nest in a cavity or on a cliff that is well protected from the weather. Young hatch at different times, so some leave the nest before others. Doesn't nest in the Dakotas.

female
p. 139

male

Rose-breasted Grosbeak
Pheucticus ludovicianus

SUMMER
MIGRATION

Size: 7–8" (18–20 cm)

Male: Plump black-and-white bird with a large triangular, rose-colored patch on the breast. Wing linings are rose red. Large ivory bill.

Female: heavily streaked with obvious white eyebrows and orange-to-yellow wing linings

Juvenile: similar to female

Nest: cup; female and male construct; 1–2 broods per year

Eggs: 3–5; blue-green with brown markings

Incubation: 13–14 days; female and male incubate

Fledging: 9–12 days; female and male feed the young

Migration: complete, to Mexico, Central America and South America

Food: insects, seeds, fruit; comes to seed feeders

Compare: Male is very distinctive, with no look-alikes. Look for the rose breast patch to identify.

Stan's Notes: A summer resident, but more conspicuous when in small groups during spring and autumn migrations. Prefers a mature deciduous forest for nesting. Both sexes sing, but the male sings much louder and clearer. Sings a rich, robin-like song with a chip note in the tune. "Grosbeak" refers to the thick, strong bill, which is used to crush seeds. The rose patch varies in size and shape in each male. Males have white wing patches that flash during flight. Males arrive at the breeding grounds a few days before the females. Several males will come to seed feeders together in spring. When the females arrive, males become territorial and reduce their feeder visits. After fledging, young grosbeaks visit feeders with the adults.

male

female

Hairy Woodpecker
Leuconotopicus villous

Size: 9" (23 cm)

Male: Black-and-white woodpecker with a white belly. Black wings with rows of white spots. White stripe down the back. Long black bill. Red mark on the back of the head.

Female: same as male but lacks the red mark

Juvenile: grayer version of the female

Nest: cavity with an oval entrance hole; female and male excavate; 1 brood per year

Eggs: 3–6; white without markings

Incubation: 11–15 days; female incubates during the day, male incubates at night

Fledging: 28–30 days; male and female feed the young

Migration: non-migrator; moves around in winter to find food

Food: insects, nuts, seeds; comes to seed and suet feeders

Compare: Downy Woodpecker (p. 51) is much smaller and has a much shorter bill. Look for Hairy Woodpecker's long bill.

Stan's Notes: A common bird in wooded backyards. Announces its arrival with a sharp chirp before landing on feeders. Responsible for eating many destructive forest insects. Uses its barbed tongue to extract insects from trees. Tiny, bristle-like feathers at the base of the bill protect the nostrils from wood dust. Drums on hollow logs, branches or stovepipes in spring to announce territory. Prefers to excavate nest cavities in live aspen trees. Excavates a larger, more oval-shaped entrance than the round entrance hole of the Downy Woodpecker. Makes short flights from tree to tree.

juvenile

Red-headed Woodpecker

Melanerpes erythrocephalus

SUMMER
MIGRATION

Size: 9" (22.5 cm)

Male: All-red head with a solid black back. White chest, belly and rump. Black wings with large white wing patches seen flashing in flight. Black tail. Gray legs and bill.

Female: same as male

Juvenile: gray brown with white chest, lacks any red

Nest: cavity; male builds with help from female; 1 brood per year

Eggs: 4–5; white without markings

Incubation: 12–13 days; female and male incubate

Fledging: 27–30 days; female and male feed the young

Migration: partial migrator to complete migrator; will move to areas with an abundant supply of nuts

Food: insects, nuts, fruit; visits suet and seed feeders

Compare: No other woodpecker in the Dakotas has an all-red head.

Stan's Notes: One of the few non-dimorphic woodpeckers, with males and females that look alike. Bill is strong enough to excavate a nest cavity only in soft, dead trees. Prefers open woodlands or woodland edges with many dead or rotting branches. Unlike other woodpeckers, which use nest cavities just once briefly, it may use the same cavity for several years in a row. Often perches on top of dead snags. Stores acorns and other nuts. Gives a shrill, hoarse "churr" call. Was once the most common of woodpeckers and now is very uncommon to rare. Population decline near 90 percent.

male

female

Red-bellied Woodpecker
Melanerpes carolinus

YEAR-ROUND

Size: 9–9½" (23–24 cm)

Male: Black-and-white "zebra-backed" woodpecker with a white rump. Red crown extends down the nape of the neck. Tan chest. Pale-red tinge on the belly, often hard to see.

Female: same as male but with a light-gray crown and a red nape

Juvenile: gray version of adults; lacks a red crown and red nape

Nest: cavity; female and male excavate; 1 brood per year

Eggs: 4–5; white without markings

Incubation: 12–14 days; female incubates during the day, male incubates at night

Fledging: 24–27 days; female and male feed the young

Migration: non-migrator; moves around to find food

Food: insects, nuts, fruit; visits suet and seed feeders

Compare: Similar to the Northern Flicker (p. 185). Look for the zebra-striped back to help identify the Red-bellied Woodpecker.

Stan's Notes: Likes shady woodlands, forest edges and backyards. Digs holes in rotten wood to find spiders, centipedes, beetles and more. Hammers acorns and berries into crevices of trees for winter food. Returns to the same tree to excavate a new nest below that of the previous year. Often kicked out of nest hole by European Starlings. Undulating flight with rapid wingbeats. Gives a loud "querrr" call and a low "chug-chug-chug." Named for the pale red tinge on its belly. Expanding its range all over the country.

female p. 187

male

Lesser Scaup
Aythya affinis

SUMMER MIGRATION

Size: 16–17" (40–43 cm)

Male: Appears mostly black with bold white sides and a gray back. Chest and head look nearly black, but head appears purple with green highlights in direct sun. Bright-yellow eyes.

Female: overall brown with a dull-white patch at the base of a light-gray bill; yellow eyes

Juvenile: same as female

Nest: ground; female builds; 1 brood per year

Eggs: 8–14; olive-buff without markings

Incubation: 22–28 days; female incubates

Fledging: 45–50 days; female teaches the young to feed

Migration: complete, to southern states, Mexico, Central America and northern South America

Food: aquatic plants and insects

Compare: Larger than American Coot (p. 41), which lacks male Scaup's white sides. The male Blue-winged Teal (p. 185) is slightly smaller, with a white crescent on its bill. The white sides and gray back help identify the male Lesser Scaup.

Stan's Notes: A summer resident in North Dakota. Seen in South Dakota during migration. A common diving duck. Submerges completely to feed on the bottom (unlike dabbling ducks, which tip forward to reach the bottom). Note the bold white stripe under the wings when in flight. The male leaves the female when she starts incubating eggs. Egg quantity (clutch size) increases with the female's age. Has an interesting babysitting arrangement: groups of young (crèches) are tended by one to three adult females.

female
p. 189

male

Ring-necked Duck
Aythya collaris

SUMMER

Size: 16–19" (41–48 cm)

Male: Striking black duck with light-gray-to-white sides. Blue bill with a bold white ring and a thinner ring at the base. Peaked head with a sloped forehead.

Female: brown with darker-brown back and crown, light-brown sides, gray face, white eye-ring, white ring around the bill, and peaked head

Juvenile: similar to female

Nest: ground; female builds; 1 brood per year

Eggs: 8–10; olive-gray to brown without markings

Incubation: 26–27 days; female incubates

Fledging: 49–56 days; female teaches the young to feed

Migration: complete, to southern states and Mexico

Food: aquatic plants and insects

Compare: Similar size as male Lesser Scaup (p. 65), which has a gray back unlike the black back of male Ring-necked Duck. Look for the blue bill with a bold white ring to identify the male Ring-necked Duck.

Stan's Notes: Usually in larger freshwater lakes rather than marshes, in small flocks or just pairs. Watch for this diving duck to dive underwater to forage for food. Springs up off the water to take flight. Flattens its crown when diving. Male gives a quick series of grating barks and grunts. Female gives high-pitched peeps. Named "Ring-necked" for its cinnamon collar, which is nearly impossible to see in the field. Also called Ring-billed Duck due to the white ring on its bill.

winter

breeding

American Avocet
Recurvirostra americana

Size: 18" (45 cm)

Male: Black-and-white back, with a white belly. A long, thin upturned bill and long gray legs. Rusty-red head and neck during breeding season, gray in winter.

Female: similar to male, more strongly upturned bill

Juvenile: similar to adults, slight wash of rusty red on the neck and head

Nest: ground; female and male construct; 1 brood per year

Eggs: 3–5; light olive with brown markings

Incubation: 22–29 days; female and male incubate

Fledging: 28–35 days; female and male feed young

Migration: complete, to southwestern states, Mexico

Food: insects, crustaceans, aquatic vegetation, fruit

Compare: One of the few long-legged shorebirds in the Dakotas. Look for the rusty-red head of breeding Avocet and the long upturned bill.

Stan's Notes: A handsome, long-legged bird that prefers shallow alkaline, saline or brackish water, it is well adapted to arid western U.S. conditions. Uses its upturned bill to sweep from side to side across mud bottoms in search of insects. Both the male and female have a brood patch to incubate eggs and brood their young. Nests throughout the Dakotas in loose colonies of up to 20 pairs; all members defend against intruders together.

female
p. 197

male

Common Goldeneye
Bucephala clangula

Size: 18–20" (45–51 cm)

Male: Mostly white duck with a black back and a large, puffy, green head. Large white spot on the face. Bright-golden eyes. Dark bill.

Female: large dark-brown head with a gray body and a white collar, bright-golden eyes, yellow-lipped dark bill

Juvenile: same as female but has dark eyes

Nest: cavity; female lines an old woodpecker cavity; 1 brood per year

Eggs: 8–10; light green without markings

Incubation: 28–32 days; female incubates

Fledging: 56–59 days; female leads the young to food

Migration: complete to southern states and Mexico; winters in parts of the Dakotas

Food: aquatic plants, insects, fish, mollusks

Compare: The black-and-white male Lesser Scaup (p. 65) is similar but smaller. American Coot (p. 41) is smaller and lacks the bright-golden eyes and white spot in front of each eye.

Stan's Notes: Known for the loud whistling sound produced by its wings during flight. During late winter and early spring, the male performs elaborate mating displays that include throwing his head back and calling a raspy note. The female will lay some of her eggs in other goldeneye nests or in the nests of other species (called egg dumping), causing some mothers to incubate as many as 30 eggs in a brood. Named for its bright-golden eyes. Winters in the Dakotas wherever it finds open water.

Black-billed Magpie
Pica hudsonia

YEAR-ROUND

Size: 20" (50 cm)

Male: Large black-and-white bird with a very long tail and white belly. Iridescent green wings and tail in direct sunlight. Large black bill. Black legs. White wing patches flash in flight.

Female: same as male

Juvenile: same as adult, but has a shorter tail

Nest: modified pendulous; male and female build; 1 brood per year

Eggs: 5–8; green with brown markings

Incubation: 16–21 days; female incubates

Fledging: 25–29 days; female and male feed young

Migration: non-migrator

Food: insects, carrion, fruit, seeds

Compare: Larger than the Common Grackle (p. 37). The contrasting black-and-white colors and the very long tail of the Black-billed Magpie distinguish it from the all-black American Crow (p. 43).

Stan's Notes: A wonderfully intelligent bird that is able to mimic dogs, cats and even people. Will often raid a barnyard dog dish for food. Feeds on a variety of food from roadkill to insects and seeds it collects from the ground. Easily identified by its bold black-and-white colors and long streaming tail. Travels in small flocks, usually family members, and tends to be very gregarious. Breeds in small colonies. Unusual dome nest (dome-shaped roof) deep within thick shrubs. Mates with same mate for several years. Prefers open fields with cattle or sheep, where it feeds on insects attracted to livestock.

soaring

Osprey
Pandion haliaetus

SUMMER
MIGRATION

Size: 21–24" (53–61 cm); up to 5½' wingspan

Male: Large eagle-like bird with a white chest, belly and head. Dark eye line. Nearly black back. Black "wrist" marks on the wings. Dark bill.

Female: same as male but slightly larger and with a necklace of brown streaks

Juvenile: similar to adults, with a light-tan breast

Nest: platform on a raised wooden platform, man-made tower or tall dead tree; female and male build; 1 brood per year

Eggs: 2–4; white with brown markings

Incubation: 32–42 days; female and male incubate

Fledging: 48–58 days; male and female feed the young

Migration: complete, to southern states and Mexico

Food: fish

Compare: The juvenile Bald Eagle (p. 81) is brown with white speckles. The adult Bald Eagle has an all-white head and tail. Look for the white belly and dark eye line to identify the Osprey.

Stan's Notes: The only species in its family, and the only raptor that plunges into water feetfirst to catch fish. Always near water. Can hover for a few seconds before diving. Carries fish in a head-first position for better aerodynamics. Wings angle back in flight. Often harassed by Bald Eagles for its catch. Gives a high-pitched, whistle-like call, often calling in flight as a warning. Mates have a long-term pair bond. May not migrate to the same wintering grounds. Was nearly extinct but is now doing well.

in flight

juvenile

Black-crowned Night-Heron
Nycticorax nycticorax

SUMMER
MIGRATION

Size: 22–27" (56–69 cm); up to 3½' wingspan

Male: A stocky, hunched and inactive heron with black back and crown, white belly and gray wings. Long dark bill and bright-red eyes. Short dull-yellow legs. Breeding adult has 2 long white plumes on crown.

Female: same as male

Juvenile: golden-brown head and back with white spots, streaked breast, yellow-orange eyes, brown bill

Nest: platform; female and male build; 1 brood per year

Eggs: 3–5; light blue without markings

Incubation: 24–26 days; female and male incubate

Fledging: 42–48 days; female and male feed the young

Migration: complete, to southern states, Mexico and Central America

Food: fish, aquatic insects

Compare: American Bittern (p. 217) is overall brown and has a yellow bill. A perching Great Blue Heron (p. 275) looks twice the size of a Black-crowned. Look for a short-necked heron with a black back and crown.

Stan's Notes: A very secretive bird, this heron is most active near dawn and dusk (crepuscular). It hunts alone, but it nests in small colonies. Roosts in trees during the day. Often squawks if disturbed from the daytime roost. Often seen being harassed by other herons during days. Stalks quiet backwaters in search of small fish and crabs.

rushing

weed dance

Western Grebe
Aechmophorus occidentalis

Size: 24" (60 cm)

Male: Long-necked, nearly all-black waterbird. White chin, neck, chest and belly. Long greenish-yellow bill. Bright-red eyes. Dark crown extends around eyes to base of bill. In winter, becomes light gray around eyes.

Female: same as male

Juvenile: similar to adult

Nest: platform; female and male construct; 1 brood per year

Eggs: 3–4; bluish white with brown markings

Incubation: 20–23 days; female and male incubate

Fledging: 65–75 days; female and male feed young

Migration: complete, to wesstern coastal U.S.

Food: fish, aquatic insects

Compare: A familiar long-necked waterbird. Striking black-and-white plumage makes it hard to confuse with any other bird.

Stan's Notes: Well known for its unusual breeding dance, called rushing. Side by side with necks outstretched, mates spring to their webbed feet and dance across the water's surface (see inset). Often holds long stalks of water plants in bill when courting (weed dance, see inset). Its legs are positioned far back on the body, making it difficult to walk on ground. Shortly after choosing a large lake for breeding, it rarely flies until late in summer. Young ride on backs of adults, climbing on minutes after hatching. Nests in large colonies of up to 100 pairs on lakes with tall vegetation.

soaring

juvenile

soaring
juvenile

Bald Eagle

Haliaeetus leucocephalus

YEAR-ROUND
WINTER

Size: 31–37" (79–94 cm); up to 7½' wingspan

Male: White head and tail contrast sharply with the dark-brown-to-black body and wings. Large, curved yellow bill and yellow feet.

Female: same as male but larger

Juvenile: dark brown with white speckles and spots on the body and wings; gray bill

Nest: massive platform, usually in a tree; female and male build; 1 brood per year

Eggs: 2–3; off-white without markings

Incubation: 34–36 days; female and male incubate

Fledging: 75–90 days; female and male feed the young

Migration: partial to non-migrator, to southern states; moves around to find open water and food

Food: fish, carrion, birds (mainly ducks)

Compare: The Turkey Vulture (p. 45) lacks the white head and white tail of adult Bald Eagle. Turkey Vulture has two-toned wings and flies with its wings in a V shape, unlike the straight-out wing position of the Eagle.

Stan's Notes: Nearly became extinct due to DDT poisoning and illegal killing. Returns to the same nest each year, adding more sticks and enlarging it to huge proportions, at times up to 1,000 pounds (450 kg). In their midair mating ritual, one eagle flips upside down and locks talons with another. Both tumble, then break apart to continue flight. Not uncommon for juveniles to perform this mating ritual even though they have not reached breeding age. Long-term pair bond but will switch mates when not successful at reproducing. Juveniles attain the white head and tail at 4–5 years of age.

Tree Swallow
Tachycineta bicolor

SUMMER

Size: 5–6" (13–15 cm)

Male: Blue-green in spring, greener in fall. Changes color in direct sunlight. White from chin to belly. Long, pointed wing tips. Notched tail.

Female: similar to male but duller

Juvenile: gray-brown with a white belly and a grayish breast band

Nest: cavity; female and male line a vacant woodpecker cavity or nest box; 2 broods per year

Eggs: 4–6; white without markings

Incubation: 13–16 days; female incubates

Fledging: 20–24 days; female and male feed the young

Migration: complete, to southern states, Mexico and Central America

Food: insects

Compare: Purple Martin (p. 93) male is similar in color, but it is larger and lacks a white chest and belly. The Barn Swallow (p. 87) has a rusty belly and a long, deeply forked tail.

Stan's Notes: Most common along ponds, lakes and agricultural fields. Can be attracted to your yard with a nest box. Competes with Eastern Bluebirds for cavities and nest boxes. Builds a grass nest within and will travel long distances, looking for dropped feathers for the lining. Watch for it playing and chasing after feathers. Flies with rapid wingbeats, then glides. Gives a series of gurgles and chirps. Chatters when upset or threatened. Eats many nuisance bugs. Gathers in large flocks to migrate.

female
p. 115

male

Lazuli Bunting
Passerina amoena

SUMMER MIGRATION

Size: 5½" (14 cm)

Male: A turquoise-blue head, neck, back and tail. Cinnamon chest with cinnamon extending down flanks slightly. White belly. Two bold white wing bars. Non-breeding male has a spotty blue head and back.

Female: overall grayish brown, warm-brown breast, a light wash of blue on wings and tail, gray throat, light-gray belly and 2 narrow white wing bars

Juvenile: similar to adult of the same sex

Nest: cup; female builds; 2–3 broods per year

Eggs: 3–5; pale blue without markings

Incubation: 11–13 days; female incubates

Fledging: 10–12 days; female and male feed young

Migration: complete, to Mexico

Food: insects, seeds

Compare: The male Eastern Bluebird (p. 89) is larger, darker blue, has a darker-brown breast and lacks white wing bars.

Stan's Notes: This bunting is more common in the western half of the Dakotas. Strong association with water such as rivers and streams. Gathers in small flocks after breeding to hunt for insects and look for seeds. Has increased in population and expanded its range over the last century. Males sing from short shrubs and scrubby areas to attract females. Rarely perches on tall trees. Each male has his own unique combination of notes to produce his "own" song.

Barn Swallow
Hirundo rustica

Size: 7" (18 cm)

Male: Sleek swallow. Blue-black back, cinnamon belly and reddish-brown chin. White spots on a long, deeply forked tail.

Female: same as male but with a whitish belly

Juvenile: similar to adults, with a tan belly and chin, and shorter tail

Nest: cup; female and male build; 2 broods per year

Eggs: 4–5; white with brown markings

Incubation: 13–17 days; female incubates

Fledging: 18–23 days; female and male feed the young

Migration: complete, to South America

Food: insects (prefers beetles, wasps, flies)

Compare: Cliff Swallow (p. 117) is smaller and lacks a distinctive, deeply forked tail. The Chimney Swift (p. 99) has a narrow pointed tail with wings longer than the body. Purple Martin (p. 93) is nearly 2 inches (5 cm) larger and has a dark-purple belly. Look for Barn Swallow's deeply forked tail.

Stan's Notes: Seen in wetlands, farms, suburban yards and parks. Of the six swallow species regularly found in the Dakotas, this is the only one with a deeply forked tail. Unlike other swallows, it rarely glides in flight. Usually flies low over land or water. Drinks as it flies, skimming water, or will sip water droplets on wet leaves. Bathes while flying through rain or sprinklers. Gives a twittering warble, followed by a mechanical sound. Builds a mud nest with up to 1,000 beak-loads of mud. Nests on barns and houses, under bridges and in other sheltered places. Often nests in colonies of 4–6 birds; sometimes nests alone.

male

female

Eastern Bluebird
Sialia sialis

YEAR-ROUND
SUMMER

Size: 7" (18 cm)

Male: Sky-blue head, back and tail. Rust-red breast and white belly.

Female: grayer than male, with a faint rusty breast and faint blue wings and tail

Juvenile: similar to female but with spots on the breast and blue wing markings

Nest: cavity, vacant woodpecker cavity or nest box; female adds a soft lining; 2 broods per year

Eggs: 4–5; pale blue without markings

Incubation: 12–14 days; female incubates

Fledging: 15–18 days; male and female feed the young

Migration: complete, to southern states

Food: insects, fruit; comes to shallow dishes with live or dead mealworms, and to suet feeders

Compare: Mountain Bluebird (p. 91) is the same size but lacks Eastern's rusty red breast. Blue Jay (p. 95) is considerably larger, with a crest and white markings.

Stan's Notes: A summer resident of open fields and agricultural areas, gathering in lage family groups for migration. Once nearly eliminated from the Dakotas due to a lack of nest cavities. Thanks to people who installed thousands of nest boxes, bluebirds now thrive. Prefers open habitats, such as farm fields, pastures and roadsides, but also likes forest edges, parks and yards. Easily tamed. Often perches on trees or fence posts and drops to the ground to grab bugs, especially grasshoppers. Makes short flights from tree to tree. Song is a distinctive "churlee chur chur-lee." The rust-red breast is like that of the American Robin, its cousin.

male

female

Mountain Bluebird
Sialia currucoides

SUMMER
MIGRATION

Size: 7" (18 cm)

Male: Overall sky-blue bird with a darker blue head, back, wings and tail. White lower belly. Thin black bill.

Female: similar to male, but paler with a nearly gray head and chest and a whitish belly

Juvenile: similar to adult of the same sex

Nest: cavity, old woodpecker cavity, wooden nest box; female builds; 1–2 broods per year

Eggs: 4–6; pale blue without markings

Incubation: 13 14 days; female incubates

Fledging: 22–23 days; female and male feed young

Migration: complete, to Arizona, California and Mexico

Food: insects, fruit

Compare: Similar to Eastern Bluebird (p. 89) but lacks Eastern's rusty red breast.

Stan's Notes: Common in open country, nesting in the western Dakotas. Main diet is insects. Often hovers just before diving to the ground to grab an insect. Due to conservation of suitable nesting sites (dead trees with cavities and man-made nest boxes), populations have increased over the past 40 years. Like other bluebirds, Mountain Bluebirds take well to nest boxes and tolerate close contact with people. Female sits on baby birds (brood) for up to six days after the eggs hatch. Young imprint on their first nest box or cavity and then choose a similar type of box or cavity throughout their life. Any open field is a good place to look for Mountain Bluebirds.

male

female

Purple Martin
Progne subis

SUMMER MIGRATION

Size: 8½" (21.5 cm)

Male: Iridescent with a purple-to-black head, back and belly. Black wings and a notched black tail.

Female: grayish-purple head and back, darker wings and tail, whitish belly

Juvenile: same as female

Nest: cavity; female and male line the cavity of the house; 1 brood per year

Eggs: 4–5; white without markings

Incubation: 15–18 days; female incubates

Fledging: 26–30 days; male and female feed the young

Migration: complete, to South America

Food: insects

Compare: Usually seen only in groups. The male Purple Martin is the only swallow with a very dark-purplish belly.

Stan's Notes: The largest swallow species in North America. Once nested in tree cavities; now nests almost exclusively in man-made, apartment-style houses. The most successful colonies often nest in multiunit nest boxes within 100 feet (30 m) of a human dwelling near a lake. Main diet consists of dragonflies, not mosquitoes, as once thought. Gives a continuous stream of chirps, creaks and rattles, along with a shout-like "churrr" and chortle. Often drinks in flight, skimming water, and bathes in flight, flying through rain. Returns to the same nest site each year; the males arrive before the females and yearlings. The young leave to form new colonies. Large colonies gather in fall before migrating to South America.

Blue Jay
Cyanocitta cristata

YEAR-ROUND

Size: 12" (30 cm)

Male: Bright light-blue-and-white bird with a black necklace and gray belly. Large crest moves up and down at will. White face, wing bars and tip of tail. Black tail bands.

Female: same as male

Juvenile: same as adult but duller

Nest: cup; female and male construct; 1–2 broods per year

Eggs: 4–5; green to blue with brown markings

Incubation: 16–18 days; female incubates

Fledging: 17–21 days; female and male feed the young

Migration: non-migrator to partial migrator; will move around to find an abundant food source

Food: insects, fruit, carrion, seeds, nuts; visits seed feeders, ground feeders with corn or peanuts

Compare: Eastern Bluebird (p. 89) is much smaller and lacks the crest. The Belted Kingfisher (p. 97) lacks the vivid blue coloring and black necklace of Blue Jay.

Stan's Notes: Highly intelligent, solving problems, gathering food and communicating more than other birds. Loud and noisy; mimics other birds. Known as the alarm of the forest, screaming at intruders. Imitates hawk calls around feeders to scare off other birds. One of the few birds to cache food; can remember where it hid thousands of nuts. Carries food in a pouch under its tongue (sublingually). Eats eggs and young from other nests. Feathers lack blue pigment; refracted sunlight causes the blue appearance.

YEAR-ROUND
SUMMER

Belted Kingfisher
Megaceryle alcyon

Size: 12–14" (30–36 cm)

Male: Blue with white belly, blue-gray chest band, and black wing tips. Ragged crest moves up and down at will. Large head. Long, thick, black bill. White spot by eyes. Red-brown eyes.

Female: same as male but with rusty flanks and a rusty chest band below the blue-gray band

Juvenile: similar to female

Nest: cavity; female and male excavate in a bank of a river, lake or cliff; 1 brood per year

Eggs: 6–7; white without markings

Incubation: 23–24 days; female and male incubate

Fledging: 23–24 days; female and male feed the young

Migration: complete, to southern states, Mexico and Central and South America; doesn't migrate in some areas in South Dakota

Food: small fish

Compare: The Blue Jay (p. 95) is lighter blue and has a plain gray chest and belly. The Belted Kingfisher is rarely found away from water.

Stan's Notes: Usually found at the bank of a river, lake or large stream. Perches on a branch near water, dives in headfirst to catch a small fish, then returns to the branch to feed. Parents drop dead fish into the water to teach their young to dive. Can't pass bones through its digestive tract; regurgitates bone pellets after meals. Loud call that sounds like a machine gun. Mates know each other by their calls. Digs a tunnel up to 4 feet (about 1 m) long to a nest chamber. Small white patches on dark wing tips flash during flight.

Chimney Swift
Chaetura pelagica

SUMMER

Size: 5" (13 cm)

Male: Nondescript, cigar-shaped bird, usually seen in flight. Long, thin, brown body. Pointed tail and head. Long, backswept wings, longer than the body.

Female: same as male

Juvenile: same as adults

Nest: half cup; female and male construct; 1 brood per year

Eggs: 4–5; white without markings

Incubation: 19–21 days; female and male incubate

Fledging: 28–30 days; female and male feed the young

Migration: complete, to South America

Food: insects caught in midair

Compare: The Purple Martin (p. 93) is much larger and darker. The Barn Swallow (p. 87) has a deeply forked tail. Tree Swallows (p. 83) have a white belly and blue-green back. Look for the cigar shape to identify the Chimney Swift in flight.

Stan's Notes: One of the fastest fliers in the bird world. Spends all day flying, rarely perching. Flies in groups, feeding on insects flying 100 feet (30 m) or higher up in the air. Often called a Flying Cigar due to its body shape, which is pointed at both ends. Drinks and bathes during flight, skimming water. Gives a unique in-flight twittering call, often heard before the bird is seen. Hundreds roost in large chimneys, giving it the common name. Builds its nest with tiny twigs, cementing it with saliva and attaching it to the inside of a chimney or a hollow tree. Usually only one nest per chimney.

Common Redpoll
Acanthis flammea

WINTER

Size: 5" (13 cm)

Male: Sparrow-like bird with a bright-red crown and raspberry red on the chest. Black spot on the chin. Heavily streaked back.

Female: similar to male but lacks red on the chest

Juvenile: browner than adults, with dark streaking on the chest; lacks a red crown

Nest: cup; female builds; 1 brood (occasionally 2) per year

Eggs: 4–5; pale green with purple markings

Incubation: 10–11 days; female incubates

Fledging: 11–12 days; female and male feed the young

Migration: irruptive; moves from Canada into North and South Dakota in some winters

Food: seeds, insects; will come to seed feeders

Compare: Male Purple Finch (p. 295) is slightly larger and has a red back and rump. Male House Finch (p. 293) is similar, but it has an orange-red rump. Look for the bright-red crown and black spot under the bill to identify the male Common Redpoll.

Stan's Notes: This bird winters in the Dakotas after summering in the far reaches of Canada. Moves from location to location, wheeling around in the sky before landing at feeders. Visits feeders in small to large flocks. Flocks of up 100 birds are not uncommon but are not seen at all in some winters. Bathes in open water or snow in winter. Like the Black-capped Chickadee, it can be tamed and fed by hand. Gives a zipping call in long strings that last 30 seconds or more. Also gives a nasal, rising whistle.

Chipping Sparrow
Spizella passerina

Size: 5" (13 cm)

Male: Small gray-brown sparrow with clear-gray chest. Rusty crown. White eyebrows and thin black eye line. Thin gray-black bill. Two faint wing bars.

Female: same as male

Juvenile: similar to adults, with streaking on the chest; lacks a rusty crown

Nest: cup; female builds; 2 broods per year

Eggs: 3–5; blue-green with brown markings

Incubation: 11–14 days; female incubates

Fledging: 10–12 days; female and male feed the young

Migration: complete to southern states, Mexico and Central America

Food: insects, seeds; will come to ground feeders

Compare: Similar to American Tree Sparrow (p. 119), which shares a rusty crown but lacks dark eye line. The Lark Sparrow (p. 131) is larger and has a white chest and central spot. Song Sparrow (p. 111) and female House Finch (p. 107) have heavily streaked chests.

Stan's Notes: A common garden or yard bird, often seen feeding on dropped seeds beneath feeders. Gathers in large family groups to feed in preparation for migration. Migrates at night in flocks of 20–30 birds. The common name comes from the male's fast "chip" call. Often is just called Chippy. Builds nest low in dense shrubs and almost always lines it with animal hair. Comfortable with people, allowing you to approach closely before it flies away.

Pine Siskin
Spinus pinus

Size: 5" (13 cm)

Male: Small brown finch with heavy streaking on the back, breast and belly. Yellow wing bars. Yellow at the base of tail. Thin bill.

Female: similar to male, with less yellow

Juvenile: similar to adult, with a light-yellow tinge over the breast and chin

Nest: cup; female builds; 2 broods

Eggs: 3–4; greenish blue with brown markings

Incubation: 12–13 days; female incubates

Fledging: 14–15 days; female and male feed the young

Migration: irruptive; moves around the United States in search of food

Food: seeds, insects; will come to seed feeders

Compare: Female House Finch (p. 107) lacks any yellow. The female American Goldfinch (p. 317) has white wing bars. Female Purple Finch (p. 123) has bold white eyebrows. Look for the yellow wing bars to identify the Pine Siskin.

Stan's Notes: Usually considered a winter finch, seen in flocks of up to 20 birds, often with other finch species. While it can be found throughout the Dakotas in heavy invasion years, it is absent in many winters. Will come to thistle feeders. Gives a series of high-pitched, wheezy calls. Also gives a wheezing twitter. Breeds in small groups. Builds nest toward the end of coniferous branches, where needles are dense, helping to conceal. Nests are often only a few feet apart. Male feeds the female during incubation. Juveniles lose the yellow tint by late summer of their first year.

male
p. 293

female

YEAR-ROUND

House Finch
Haemorhous mexicanus

Size: 5" (13 cm)

Female: Plain brown with heavy streaking on a white chest.

Male: red-to-orange face, throat, chest and rump, streaked belly and wings, brown cap, brown marking behind the eyes

Juvenile: similar to female

Nest: cup, occasionally in a cavity; female builds; 2 broods per year

Eggs: 4–5; pale blue, lightly marked

Incubation: 12–14 days; female incubates

Fledging: 15–19 days; female and male feed the young

Migration: non-migrator to partial migrator; will move around to find food

Food: seeds, fruit, leaf buds; visits seed feeders and feeders that offer grape jelly

Compare: The female Purple Finch (p. 123) is very similar but has bold white eyebrows. The female American Goldfinch (p. 317) has a clear chest and white wing bars. Similar to Pine Siskin (p. 105), but it lacks yellow wing bars and has a much larger bill than Siskin.

Stan's Notes: Can be a common bird at your feeders. A very social bird, visiting feeders in small flocks. Likes to nest in hanging flower baskets. Male sings a loud, cheerful warbling song. Historically it occurred from the Pacific coast to the Rockies, with only a few reaching the eastern side. Now found throughout the country. Suffers from a disease that causes the eyes to crust, resulting in blindness and death.

SUMMER

House Wren
Troglodytes aedon

Size:	5" (13 cm)
Male:	All-brown bird with lighter-brown markings on the wings and tail. Slightly curved brown bill. Often holds tail upward.
Female:	same as male
Juvenile:	same as adult
Nest:	cavity; female and male line just about any nest cavity; 2 broods per year
Eggs:	4–6; tan with brown markings
Incubation:	10–13 days; female and male incubate
Fledging:	12–15 days; female and male feed the young
Migration:	complete, to southern states and Mexico
Food:	insects, spiders, snails
Compare:	Wren's long curved bill and long upturned tail differentiates it from sparrows. Lack of eyebrows distinguishes it from other wrens.

Stan's Notes: A prolific songster. During the mating season, sings from dawn to dusk. Seen in brushy yards, parks and woodlands and along forest edges. Easily attracted to a nest box. In spring, the male chooses several prospective nesting cavities and places a few small twigs in each. The female inspects all of them and finishes constructing the nest in the cavity of her choice. She fills the cavity with short twigs and then lines a small depression at the back with pine needles and grass. She often has trouble fitting longer twigs through the entrance hole and tries many different directions and approaches until she is successful.

Song Sparrow
Melospiza melodia

YEAR-ROUND
SUMMER

Size: 5–6" (13–15 cm)

Male: Common brown sparrow with heavy dark streaks on the chest coalescing into a central dark spot.

Female: same as male

Juvenile: similar to adults, with a finely streaked chest; lacks a central dark spot

Nest: cup; female builds; 2 broods per year

Eggs: 3–4; blue to green, with red-brown markings

Incubation: 12–14 days; female incubates

Fledging: 9–12 days; female and male feed the young

Migration: complete, to southern states; non-migrator in South Dakota and southern North Dakota

Food: insects, seeds; only rarely comes to ground feeders with seeds

Compare: Similar to other brown sparrows. Look for the heavily streaked chest with a central dark spot to help identify the Song Sparrow.

Stan's Notes: There are many subspecies of this bird, but the dark spot in the center of the chest appears in every variety. A constant songster, repeating its loud, clear song every few minutes. The song varies from region to region but has the same basic structure. Sings from thick shrubs to defend a small territory, beginning with three notes and finishing up with a trill. A ground feeder, it will "double-scratch" with both feet at the same time to expose seeds. When the female builds a new nest for a second brood, the male often takes over feeding the first brood. Unlike many other sparrow species, Song Sparrows rarely flock together. A common host of the Brown-headed Cowbird.

male
p. 233

female

Dark-eyed Junco
Junco hyemalis

WINTER

Size:	5½" (14 cm)
Female:	A plump, dark-eyed bird with a tan-to-brown chest, head and back. White belly. Ivory-to-pink bill. White outer tail feathers appear like a white V in flight.
Male:	round bird with gray plumage
Juvenile:	similar to female, with streaking on the breast and head
Nest:	cup; female and male build; 2 broods per year
Eggs:	3–5; white with reddish-brown markings
Incubation:	12–13 days; female incubates
Fledging:	10–13 days; male and female feed the young
Migration:	complete, throughout the U.S.; winters in the Dakotas
Food:	seeds, insects; visits ground and seed feeders
Compare:	Rarely confused with any other bird. Look for the ivory-to-pink bill and small flocks feeding beneath seed feeders to help identify the female Dark-eyed Junco.

Stan's Notes: Common in winter, this bird is usually seen on the ground in small flocks. Adheres to a rigid social hierarchy, with dominant birds chasing the less dominant birds. Look for the white outer tail feathers flashing in flight. Most comfortable on the ground, where it uses its feet to simultaneously "double-scratch" to expose seeds and insects. Eats many weed seeds. Several subspecies of Dark-eyed Junco were previously considered to be separate species but have now been combined into one. Doesn't nest in the Dakotas.

female

male
p. 85

Lazuli Bunting

Passerina amoena

SUMMER
MIGRATION

Size:	5½" (14 cm)
Female:	Overall grayish brown with a warm brown chest, light wash of blue on wings and tail, gray throat and light-gray belly. Two narrow white wing bars.
Male:	turquoise-blue head, neck, back and tail, cinnamon breast, white belly, 2 bold white wing bars
Juvenile:	similar to adult of the same sex
Nest:	cup; female builds; 2–3 broods per year
Eggs:	3–5; pale blue without markings
Incubation:	11–13 days; female incubates
Fledging:	10–12 days; female and male feed the young
Migration:	complete, to Mexico
Food:	insects, seeds
Compare:	Female Mountain Bluebird (p. 91) is larger and has much more blue than female bunting.

Stan's Notes: This bunting is more common in the western half of the Dakotas. Doesn't like dense forests. Strong association with water such as rivers and streams. Gathers in small flocks after breeding to hunt for insects and look for seeds. Has increased in population and expanded its range over the last century. Males sing from short shrubs and scrubby areas to attract females. Rarely perches on tall trees. Each male has his own unique combination of notes to produce his "own" song.

SUMMER

Cliff Swallow
Petrochelidon pyrrhonota

Size: 5½" (14 cm)

Male: Uniquely patterned swallow with a dark back, wings and cap. Distinctive tan-to-rust rump, cheeks and forehead.

Female: same as male

Juvenile: similar to adult, lacks distinct patterning

Nest: gourd-shaped, made of mud; male and female build; 1–2 broods per year

Eggs: 4–6; pale white with brown markings

Incubation: 14–16 days; male and female incubate

Fledging: 21–24 days; female and male feed young

Migration: complete, to South America

Food: insects

Compare: Barn Swallow (p. 87) is larger and has a distinctive, deeply forked tail and blue back and wings. Tree Swallow (p. 83) lacks any tan-to-rust coloring.

Stan's Notes: A common and widespread swallow species in the Dakotas during the summer. Common around bridges (especially bridges over water) and rural housing (especially in open country near cliffs). Builds a gourd-shaped nest with a funnel-like entrance pointing down. A colony nester, with many nests lined up beneath building eaves or cliff overhangs. Will carry balls of mud up to a mile to construct its nest. Many in the colony return to the same nest site each year. Not unusual to have two broods per season. If the number of nests underneath eaves becomes a problem, wait until the young have left the nests to hose off the mud.

American Tree Sparrow
Spizelloides arborea

MIGRATION
WINTER

Size: 6" (15 cm)

Male: Brown with a tan chest and rusty crown and eye line. Gray eyebrows. Dark spot in the center of the chest. Dark upper bill; yellow lower bill. 2 white wing bars.

Female: same as male

Juvenile: streaked chest often obscures the central dark spot; lacks a rusty crown

Nest: cup; female builds; 1 brood per year

Eggs: 3–5; greenish white with brown markings

Incubation: 12–13 days; female incubates

Fledging: 8–10 days; female and male feed the young

Migration: complete, across North America; winters in the Dakotas

Food: insects, seeds; visits seed feeders

Compare: The Chipping Sparrow (p. 103) has white eyebrows and a black eye line. The Song Sparrow (p. 111) has a heavily streaked chest. To identify the American Tree Sparrow, check for the dark spot on the chest and the two-toned bill.

Stan's Notes: Commonly seen during spring and fall migrations in flocks of 2–200 birds. A regular winter bird feeder visitor in the Dakotas. Found in open fields, woodlands and suburban backyards. Sometimes called a Winter Chippy because it looks like the Chipping Sparrow, a summer visitor. Gives a series of high-pitched, sweet-sounding whistles. Nests in Canada and Alaska. The species name *arborea* means "tree," but it doesn't nest in trees; it nests on the ground in a clump of grass. The "Tree" in the name refers to its habitat. "American" refers to its natural range.

119

House Sparrow
Passer domesticus

YEAR-ROUND

Size: 6" (15 cm)

Male: Brown back with a gray belly and cap. Large black patch extending from the throat to the chest (bib). One white wing bar.

Female: slightly smaller than the male; light brown with light eyebrows; lacks a bib and white wing bar

Juvenile: similar to female

Nest: cavity; female and male build a domed cup nest within; 2–3 broods per year

Eggs: 4–6; white with brown markings

Incubation: 10–12 days; female incubates

Fledging: 14–17 days; female and male feed the young

Migration: non-migrator; moves around to find food

Food: seeds, insects, fruit; comes to seed feeders

Compare: American Tree Sparrow (p. 119) and Chipping Sparrow (p. 103) both have rusty-red crowns. Harris's Sparrow (p. 147) has a black "hood" and white chest. Look for the black bib to identify the male House Sparrow and the clear breast to help identify the female.

Stan's Notes: One of the first birdsongs heard in cities in spring. A familiar city bird, nearly always in small flocks. Also found on farms. Introduced in 1850 from Europe to Central Park in New York. Now seen throughout North America. Related to old-world sparrows; not a relative of any sparrows in the U.S. An aggressive bird that will kill young birds in order to take over the nest cavity. Uses dried grass and small scraps of plastic, paper and other materials to build an oversize, domed nest in the cavity.

male
p. 295

female

Purple Finch
Haemorhous purpureus

MIGRATION
WINTER

Size: 6" (15 cm)

Female: plain brown with heavy streaking on the chest, bold white eyebrows and a large bill

Male: raspberry-red head, cap, breast, back and rump; brownish wings and tail

Juvenile: same as female

Nest: cup; female and male build; 1 brood per year

Eggs: 4–5; greenish blue with brown markings

Incubation: 12–13 days; female incubates

Fledging: 13–14 days; female and male feed the young

Migration: irruptive; moves around in search of food

Food: seeds, insects, fruit; comes to seed feeders

Compare: The female House Finch (p. 107) lacks eyebrows. The Pine Siskin (p. 105) has yellow wing bars. The female American Goldfinch (p. 317) has a clear chest. Look for the bold white eyebrows to identify the female Purple Finch.

Stan's Notes: Usually only seen in the winter or during migration, when Purple Finches leave their northern homes and move around in search of food. Travels in flocks of up to 50 birds. Visits seed feeders along with House Finches, which makes it hard to tell them apart. Feeds mainly on seeds; ash tree seeds are an important source of food. Found in coniferous forests, mixed woods, woodland edges and suburban backyards. Flies in the typical undulating, up-and-down pattern of finches. Sings a rich, loud song. Gives a distinctive "tic" note only in flight. The male is not purple. The Latin species name *purpureus* means "purple" (and other reddish colors).

breeding
male

female

Chestnut-collared Longspur

Calcarius ornatus

SUMMER
MIGRATION

Size: 6" (15 cm)

Male: Male breeding plumage (March to September) is overall brown. Head striped with black and white. Rusty red nape "collar." Dull-yellow throat. Black chest and belly. Small pointed bill. Winter male is much duller and lacks black head stripes, black chest and belly and red nape.

Female: similar to winter male, lacks the black and white head, black chest and belly, red nape

Juvenile: similar to female, but duller

Nest: cup; female builds; 1–2 broods per year

Eggs: 3–6; white with brown markings

Incubation: 10–13 days; female incubates

Fledging: 9–14 days; male and female feed young

Migration: complete, to Texas and Mexico

Food: insects, seeds

Compare: The Lapland Longspur (p. 127) is a winter visitor, while the Chestnut-collared visits in summer. The rusty red nape and black belly help to easily identify this grassland bird.

Stan's Notes: This bird is found in grasslands and native prairies throughout the Dakotas. Common name "Longspur" refers to the long rear toe and nail, which are nearly twice the length of the front two toes. The nest is well concealed in a shallow depression under dense vegetation on the ground, with the rim of nest flush with the ground. Male performs a mating flight with rapid wing-beats and a soft song. Adults eat insects and seeds. Young are fed an insect diet. One of four longspur species in North America.

breeding male

winter male

female

Lapland Longspur

Calcarius lapponicus

MIGRATION
WINTER

Size: 6¼" (15.5 cm)

Male: Breeding male (March to September) is overall brown with a black head, throat and chest. Tan eyebrows. Rusty red nape. White belly. Small, pointed yellow bill with a black tip. Winter male is much duller and lacks the black head, throat and chest.

Female: very similar to winter male

Juvenile: similar to female, but duller

Nest: cup; female builds; 1 brood per year

Eggs: 3–7; pale green with brown markings

Incubation: 12–13 days; female incubates

Fledging: 8–10 days; male and female feed young

Migration: complete, to central states from the East to West coasts

Food: insects, seeds

Compare: The Chestnut-collared Longspur (p. 125) is a summer visitor, while the Lapland visits in winter.

Stan's Notes: Common winter bird in the Dakotas, usually found in open areas and along roads. Often seen in flocks with Horned Larks and Snow Buntings. Common name "Longspur" refers to the long rear toe and nail, which are nearly twice the length of the front two toes. Nests in a shallow depression on the ground in Alaska and Northwest Territories of Canada. One of the widest breeding ranges, extending around the world just south of the polar region (circumpolar). One of four longspur species in North America.

male
p. 53

female

non-breeding
male

Lark Bunting
Calamospiza melanocorys

Size: 6½" (16 cm)

Female: Brown bird with heavily streaked chest and a white belly. Black vertical line on each side of white chin. May have a central dark spot on the chest. Faint white eyebrows.

Male: black bird with a large, broad head, white wing patches and large bluish-gray bill

Juvenile: similar to adult of the same sex

Nest: cup; female builds; 1–2 broods per year

Eggs: 4–6; pale blue with markings

Incubation: 11–13 days; female and male incubate

Fledging: 8–12 days; female and male feed young

Migration: complete, to southwestern states and Mexico

Food: insects, seeds

Compare: Appears similar to open-country sparrows. The female Red-winged Blackbird (p. 153) lacks the white belly and chin.

Stan's Notes: Common throughout, but is more abundant in the western third of the Dakotas in dry plains and sagebrush regions. Has short rounded wings. Flying with shallow wingbeats, the male flashes white wing patches. Male takes to air to display to female, setting its wings in a V position and floating back, rocking like a butterfly, singing a most amazing song. Song is like the song of Old World larks, hence the common name. Will flock with hundreds, if not thousands, of other Lark Buntings in autumn for migration.

Lark Sparrow
Chondestes grammacus

Size: 6½" (16 cm)

Male: All-brown bird with unique rust-red, white and black head pattern. A white breast with a central black spot. Gray rump and white edges to gray tail, as seen in flight.

Female: same as male

Juvenile: similar to adult, but no rust-red on head

Nest: cup, on the ground; female builds; 1 brood per year

Eggs: 3–6; pale white with brown markings

Incubation: 10–12 days; male and female incubate

Fledging: 10–12 days; female and male feed young

Migration: complete, to coastal Mexico and Central America

Food: seeds, insects

Compare: The White-throated Sparrow (p. 133) and White-crowned Sparrow (p. 135) both lack the Lark Sparrow's rust-red pattern on the head and central spot on a white chest. Larger than Chipping Sparrow (p. 103) has a similar rusty color on head, but it is smaller and lacks Lark Sparrow's white breast and central spot.

Stan's Notes: One of the larger sparrow species and one of the best songsters, also well known for its courtship strutting, chasing and lark-like flight pattern (rapid wingbeats with tail spread). A bird of open fields, pastures and prairies, found throughout the Dakotas but more abundant in western half. Very common during migration, when large flocks congregate. Will use nest for several years if first brood is successful.

white-striped

tan-striped

White-throated Sparrow
Zonotrichia albicollis

Size: 6–7" (15–18 cm)

Male: Brown with a gray or tan chest and belly. White or tan throat patch and eyebrows. Bold striping on the head. Small yellow spot in the space between the eye and bill, called the lore.

Female: same as male

Juvenile: similar to adults, with a heavily streaked chest and a gray throat and eyebrows

Nest: cup; female builds; 1 brood per year

Eggs: 4–6; green to blue, or cream-white with red-brown markings

Incubation: 11–14 days; female incubates

Fledging: 10–12 days; female and male feed the young

Migration: complete, to southern states and Mexico

Food: insects, seeds, fruit; visits ground feeders

Compare: White-crowned Sparrow (p. 135) lacks yellow lore and white or tan throat patch. The Lark Sparrow (p. 131) has a rust-red pattern on the head and central black spot on a white chest.

Stan's Notes: Two color variations (polymorphic): white-striped and tan-striped. Studies indicate that the white-striped adults tend to mate with the tan-striped birds; it's not clear why. Known for its wonderful song; it sings all year and can even be heard at night. White- and tan-striped males and white-striped females sing, but tan-striped females do not. No indication why. Seen during migration, often at ground feeders. Often associated with other sparrows in winter. Builds nest on the ground under small trees in bogs and coniferous forests. Doesn't nest in the Dakotas.

juvenile

White-crowned Sparrow
Zonotrichia leucophrys

MIGRATION

Size: 6½–7½" (16.5–19 cm)

Male: Brown with a gray chest and black-and-white striped crown. Small, thin, pink bill.

Female: same as male

Juvenile: similar to adults, with black and brown stripes on the head

Nest: cup; female builds; 2 broods per year

Eggs: 3–5; greenish to bluish to whitish with red-brown markings

Incubation: 11–14 days; female incubates

Fledging: 8–12 days; male and female feed the young

Migration: complete, to southern states and Mexico

Food: insects, seeds, berries; visits ground feeders

Compare: The White-throated Sparrow (p. 133) has a white or tan throat patch, and yellow spot between the eyes and bill, with a blackish bill. Lark Sparrow (p. 131) has a rust-red pattern on the head and a central black spot on a white breast.

Stan's Notes: Often in groups of up to 20 birds during migrations, when it can be seen feeding underneath seed feeders. This ground feeder will "double-scratch" backward with both feet simultaneously to find seeds. The males are prolific songsters, singing in late winter while migrating north. Males take most of the responsibility for raising the young while females start their second broods. Only 9–12 days separate the broods. Doesn't nest in the Dakotas.

Swainson's Thrush
Catharus ustulatus

SUMMER MIGRATION

Size: 7" (18 cm)

Male: Dusty brown head, back and wings. Brown smudges and spots, especially on its throat, chest and off-white belly. A small, thin two-toned bill, yellow under and black above.

Female: same as male

Juvenile: overall lighter than adult, with less distinct spots on chest

Nest: cup; female builds; 1 brood per year

Eggs: 3–5; pale blue with brown markings

Incubation: 12–14 days; female incubates

Fledging: 10–14 days; female and male feed young

Migration: complete, to Mexico, Central America and South America

Food: insects, fruit

Compare: Similar shape as American Robin (p. 253), but is smaller and lacks the red breast.

Stan's Notes: A common thrush during spring and fall migrations, and a summer resident in parts of the Dakotas. Often is hard to see because most of the time it stays on the ground in thick vegetation. Song sounds like someone playing a flute. Feeds mostly on insects during spring and summer, adding fruit to its diet in late summer. Nests in shrubs or low in conifers, building a bulky nest consisting of grass, bark and moss, all glued together with mud.

male
p. 57

female

Rose-breasted Grosbeak
Pheucticus ludovicianus

SUMMER
MIGRATION

Size: 7–8" (18–20 cm)

Female: Plump and heavily streaked. Large, obvious white eyebrows. Large ivory bill. Orange-to-yellow wing linings.

Male: black and white with a triangular rose patch in the center of the chest, rose wing linings

Juvenile: similar to female

Nest: cup; female and male construct; 1–2 broods per year

Eggs: 3–5; blue-green with brown markings

Incubation: 13–14 days; female and male incubate

Fledging: 9–12 days; female and male feed the young

Migration: complete, to Mexico, Central America and South America

Food: insects, seeds, fruit; comes to seed feeders

Compare: Looks like a large finch with bold white eyebrows and heavy streaking. The female Purple Finch (p. 123) has smaller eyebrows. The female House Finch (p. 107) lacks eyebrows.

Stan's Notes: A summer resident, but more conspicuous when in small groups during migration. Prefers a mature deciduous forest for nesting. Both sexes sing, but the male sings much louder and clearer. Sings a rich, robin-like song with a chip note in the tune. "Grosbeak" refers to the thick, strong bill, which is used to crush seeds. Males arrive at the breeding grounds a few days before females. Several males will visit seed feeders together in spring. When females arrive, males become territorial and reduce their feeder visits. After fledging, the young visit feeders with the adults. Makes short flights from tree to tree with rapid wingbeats.

female

male

Horned Lark
Eremophila alpestris

YEAR-ROUND

Size: 7–8" (18–20 cm)

Male: Tan to brown with black markings on the face. Black necklace and bill. Pale-yellow chin. Two tiny feather "horns" on the top of the head, sometimes hard to see. Dark tail with white outer tail feathers, seen in flight.

Female: duller than male; less noticeable "horns"

Juvenile: lacks a yellow chin and black markings; does not develop "horns" until the second year

Nest: ground; female builds; 2–3 broods per year

Eggs: 3–4; gray with brown markings

Incubation: 11–12 days; female incubates

Fledging: 9–12 days; female and male feed the young

Migration: non-migrator to partial in the Dakotas

Food: seeds, insects

Compare: Western Meadowlark (p. 337) is larger and has a yellow breast and belly. Look for the black markings by the eyes and the black necklace to identify the Horned Lark.

Stan's Notes: The only true lark native to North America. A year-round resident, moving around in winter to find food. Larks are a bird of open ground. Common in rural areas; often seen in large flocks. The population increased in North America over the past century as more land was cleared for farming. Male performs a fluttering courtship flight high in the air while singing a high-pitched song. Female performs a fluttering distraction display when the nest is disturbed. Starts breeding early in the year. Able to renest about a week after the brood fledges. Moves around in winter to find food. "Lark" comes from the Middle English *laverock*, or "a lark."

male
p. 25

female

Brown-headed Cowbird
Molothrus ater

SUMMER

Size: 7½" (19 cm)

Female: Dull brown with no obvious markings. Pointed, sharp, gray bill. Dark eyes.

Male: glossy black with a chocolate-brown head

Juvenile: similar to female but with dull-gray plumage and a streaked chest

Nest: no nest; lays eggs in the nests of other birds

Eggs: 5–7; white with brown markings

Incubation: 10–13 days; host birds incubate the eggs

Fledging: 10–11 days; host birds feed the young

Migration: complete, to southern states

Food: insects, seeds; will come to seed feeders

Compare: The female Red-winged Blackbird (p. 153) has white eyebrows and heavy streaking. European Starling (p. 27) has speckles and a shorter tail. The pointed gray bill helps to identify the female Brown-headed Cowbird.

Stan's Notes: Cowbirds are members of the blackbird family. Of approximately 750 species of parasitic birds worldwide, this is the only parasitic bird in the Dakotas. Brood parasites lay their eggs in the nests of other birds, leaving the host birds to raise their young. Cowbirds are known to have laid their eggs in the nests of over 200 species of birds. While some birds reject cowbird eggs, most incubate them and raise the young, even to the exclusion of their own. Look for warblers and other birds feeding young birds twice their own size. Named "Cowbird" for its habit of following bison and cattle herds to feed on insects flushed up by the animals.

juvenile

Bohemian
Waxwing

Cedar Waxwing
Bombycilla cedrorum

YEAR-ROUND
WINTER

Size: 7½" (19 cm)

Male: Sleek-looking, gray-to-brown bird. Pointed crest, bandit-like mask and light-yellow belly. Bold-yellow tip of tail. Red wing tips look like they were dipped in red wax.

Female: same as male

Juvenile: grayish with a heavily streaked breast; lacks the sleek look, black mask and red wing tips

Nest: cup; female and male construct; 1 brood per year, occasionally 2

Eggs: 4–6; pale blue with brown markings

Incubation: 10–12 days; female incubates

Fledging: 14–18 days; female and male feed the young

Migration: partial migrator; moves around to find food

Food: cedar cones, fruit, insects

Compare: Similar to its larger, less common cousin, Bohemian Waxwing (see inset). Look for the red wing tips, yellow-tipped tail and black mask to identify the Cedar Waxwing.

Stan's Notes: The name is derived from its red, wax-like wing tips and preference for the small, berry-like cones of the cedar. Seen in flocks, moving around from area to area looking for berries. Feeds on insects during summer, before berries are abundant. Wanders during winter, searching for food supplies. Year-round resident in very low numbers. Spends most of its time at the top of tall trees. Listen for the high-pitched "sreee" whistling sound it constantly makes while perched or in flight. Obtains the mask after the first year and red wing tips after the second year.

juvenile

Harris's Sparrow
Zonotrichia querula

MIGRATION WINTER

Size: 7½" (19 cm)

Male: A very large sparrow with various amounts of black on head, extending down the nape and face onto the chest. White belly. Brown back and wings. Pink bill and legs.

Female: same as male

Juvenile: similar to adult, lacks the black "hood" and spotted chest

Nest: cup, on the ground; unknown who builds; 1 brood per year

Eggs: 4–5; white with brown markings

Incubation: 13–14 days; female incubates

Fledging: 11–12 days; female and male feed young

Migration: complete, to southern states; winters in parts of South Dakota

Food: insects, seeds, berries, ground feeders

Compare: House Sparrow (p. 121) lacks the Harris's black "hood."

Stan's Notes: A large sparrow commonly seen in small groups of up to ten birds scratching under seed feeders during spring and fall migrations. Nests in northern Canada, returning to South Dakota and the central U.S. for winter. Recent studies show that a bird's status is dependent upon the amount of black on its "hood," not its age. The more black, the higher the status. Named after Edward Harris (1799–1863), a companion of John James Audubon.

winter

breeding

Spotted Sandpiper

Actitis macularius

SUMMER

Size: 8" (20 cm)

Male: Olive-brown back with black spots on a white chest and belly. White line over eyes. Long, dull-yellow legs. Long bill. Winter plumage lacks spots on the chest and belly.

Female: same as male

Juvenile: similar to winter plumage, with a darker bill

Nest: ground; male builds; 2 broods per year

Eggs: 3–4; brownish with brown markings

Incubation: 20–24 days; male incubates

Fledging: 17–21 days; male feeds the young

Migration: complete migrator, to southern states, Mexico, Central and South America

Food: aquatic insects

Compare: Lesser Yellowlegs (p. 165) is larger. Killdeer (p. 167) has 2 black neck bands. Look for the black spots on the chest and belly and the bobbing tail to help identify the breeding Spotted Sandpiper.

Stan's Notes: One of the few shorebirds that will dive underwater when pursued. Able to fly straight up out of the water. Holds wings in a cup-like arc in flight, rarely lifting them above a horizontal plane. Walks as if delicately balanced. When standing, constantly bobs its tail. Gives a rapid series of "weet-weet-weet" calls when frightened and flying away. Female mates with multiple males and lays eggs in up to five nests. Male does all of the nest building, incubating and childcare without any help from the female.

male
p. 299

female

juvenile

Northern Cardinal

Cardinalis cardinalis

YEAR-ROUND

Size: 8–9" (20–23 cm)

Female: Buff-brown with red tinges on the crest and wings. Black mask and a large reddish bill.

Male: red with a large crest and bill and a black mask extending from the face to the throat

Juvenile: same as female but with a blackish-gray bill

Nest: cup; female builds; 2–3 broods per year

Eggs: 3–4; bluish white with brown markings

Incubation: 12–13 days; female and male incubate

Fledging: 9–10 days; female and male feed the young

Migration: non-migrator

Food: seeds, insects, fruit; comes to seed feeders

Compare: The male Red Crossbill (p. 297) has dark-brown wings and a thinner crossed bill. The Cedar Waxwing (p. 145) has a small dark bill. The juvenile Northern Cardinal (bottom inset) looks like the adult female but with a dark bill. Look for the reddish bill to identify the female Northern Cardinal.

Stan's Notes: A familiar backyard bird. Seen in a variety of habitats, including parks. Usually likes thick vegetation. One of the few species in which both females and males sing. Can be heard all year. Listen for its "whata-cheer-cheer-cheer" territorial call in spring. Watch for a male feeding a female during courtship. The male also feeds the young of the first brood while the female builds a second nest. Territorial in spring, fighting its own reflection in a window or other reflective surface. Non-territorial in winter, gathering in small flocks of up to 20 birds. *Cardinalis* denotes importance, as represented by the red priestly garments of Catholic cardinals.

male
p. 31

female

Red-winged Blackbird
Agelaius phoeniceus

YEAR-ROUND
SUMMER

Size: 8½" (22 cm)

Female: Heavily streaked brown body. Pointed brown bill and white eyebrows.

Male: jet black with red-and-yellow shoulder patches (epaulets) and a pointed black bill

Juvenile: same as female

Nest: cup; female builds; 2–3 broods per year

Eggs: 3–4; bluish green with brown markings

Incubation: 10–12 days; female incubates

Fledging: 11–14 days; female and male feed the young

Migration: complete to partial migrator, to southern states, Mexico and Central America; will move around to find food

Food: seeds, insects; visits seed and suet feeders

Compare: Female Yellow-headed Blackbird (p. 163) is larger. Female Brown-headed Cowbird (p. 143) is smaller. Both species lack white eyebrows and heavily streaked chest of the female Red-winged Blackbird.

Stan's Notes: One of the most widespread and numerous birds in the Dakotas. Found around marshes, wetlands, lakes and rivers. Flocks with as many as 10,000 birds have been reported. Males arrive before females and sing to defend their territory. The male repeats his call from the top of a cattail while showing off his red-and-yellow shoulder patches. The female chooses a mate and often builds her nest over shallow water in a thick stand of cattails. The male can be aggressive when defending the nest. Feeds mostly on seeds in spring and fall, and insects throughout the summer.

male
p. 29

female

Spotted Towhee
Pipilo maculatus

Size: 8½" (22 cm)

Female: A brown head, dirty red-brown sides and a white belly. Multiple white spots on wings and sides. Long black tail with white tip. Rich red eyes.

Male: mostly black, lacking the brown head

Juvenile: brown with a heavily streaked chest

Nest: cup; female builds; 1–2 broods per year

Eggs: 3–5; white with brown markings

Incubation: 12–14 days; female and male incubate

Fledging: 10–12 days; female and male feed young

Migration: complete, to southern states

Food: seeds, fruit, insects

Compare: American Robin (p. 253) is larger. Female Rose-breasted Grosbeak (p. 139) has a streaked breast and white eyebrows.

Stan's Notes: Summer visitor in western and southern parts of the Dakotas and seen during migration. Found in a variety of habitats from thick brush and forest edges to suburban backyards. Usually heard noisily scratching through dead leaves on the ground for food. Over 70 percent of its diet is plant material. Eats more insects during spring and summer. Well known to retreat from danger by walking away rather than taking to flight. Nest is nearly always on the ground under bushes but away from where the male perches to sing. Song and plumage vary geographically and aren't well studied or understood.

female

male

Common Nighthawk
Chordeiles minor

SUMMER

Size:	9" (23 cm)
Male:	Camouflaged brown and white with a white chin. Distinctive white band across the wings and tail, seen only in flight.
Female:	similar to male, with a tan chin; lacks a white tail band
Juvenile:	similar to female
Nest:	no nest; lays eggs on the ground, usually on rocks, or on rooftop; 1 brood per year
Eggs:	2; cream with lavender markings
Incubation:	19-20 days; female and male incubate
Fledging:	20–21 days; female and male feed the young
Migration:	complete, to South America
Food:	insects caught in the air
Compare:	Chimney Swift (p. 99) is much smaller. Look for the white chin, obvious white band on the wings and characteristic flap-flap-flap-glide pattern to help identify the Common Nighthawk.

Stan's Notes: Usually only seen in flight at dusk or after sunset but not uncommon to see it sleeping on a branch during the day. A prolific insect eater and very noisy in flight, repeating a "peenting" call. Alternates slow wingbeats with bursts of quick wingbeats. In cities, prefers to nest on flat rooftops with gravel. City populations are on the decline as gravel rooftops are converted to other styles. In spring, the male performs a showy mating ritual consisting of a steep diving flight ending with a loud popping noise. One of the first birds to migrate in fall, starting in August. Often seen in large flocks.

SUMMER

Burrowing Owl
Athene cunicularia

Size: 9–10" (24 cm); up to 2' wingspan

Male: A brown owl with bold white spots and a white belly. Yellow eyes and very long legs.

Female: same as male

Juvenile: same as adult, but belly is brown

Nest: cavity, former underground mammal den; female and male line den; 1 brood per year

Eggs: 6–11; white without markings

Incubation: 26–30 days; female incubates

Fledging: 25–28 days; female and male feed young

Migration: complete, to Mexico and Central America

Food: insects, mammals, lizards, birds

Compare: Great Horned Owl (p. 213) is more than twice the size of Burrowing Owl and has feather tuft "horns." Burrowing spends most of its time on the ground, unlike tree-loving Great Horned.

Stan's Notes: An owl of fields, open backyards, golf courses and airports. Nests in large family units or in small colonies. Takes over the underground dens of mammals, occasionally widening its den by kicking dirt backward. Lines den with cow pies, horse dung, grass and feathers. Some people have had success attracting these owls to their backyards by creating artificial dens. Often seen during the day, standing or sleeping around den entrance. Male brings food to incubating female, often moving family to a new den when young are just a few weeks old. Will bob head up and down while doing deep knee bends when agitated or threatened.

in flight

juvenile

male

female

in-flight juvenile

American Kestrel
Falco sparverius

YEAR-ROUND
SUMMER

Size: 9–11" (23–28 cm); up to 2' wingspan

Male: Rust-brown back and tail. White breast with dark spots. Two vertical black lines on a white face. Blue-gray wings. Wide black band with a white edge on the tip of a rusty tail.

Female: similar to male but slightly larger, with rust-brown wings and dark bands on the tail

Juvenile: same as adult of the same sex

Nest: cavity; does not build a nest; 1 brood per year

Eggs: 4–5; white with brown markings

Incubation: 29–31 days; male and female incubate

Fledging: 30–31 days; female and male feed the young

Migration: non-migrator to partial migrator; moves around in winter

Food: insects, small mammals and birds, reptiles

Compare: The Peregrine Falcon (p. 267) is much larger and has a dark "hood" marking. No other small bird of prey has a rusty back and tail.

Stan's Notes: An unusual raptor because the sexes look different (dimorphic). Due to its small size, this falcon was once called a Sparrow Hawk. Hovers near roads, then dives for prey. Watch for it to pump its tail after landing on a perch. Perches nearly upright. Eats many grasshoppers. Adapts quickly to a wooden nest box. Can be extremely vocal, giving a loud series of high-pitched calls. Ability to see ultraviolet (UV) light helps it locate mice and other prey by their urine, which glows bright yellow in UV light.

male
p. 35

female

Yellow-headed Blackbird
Xanthocephalus xanthocephalus

SUMMER

Size:	9–11" (23–28 cm)
Female:	Large brown bird with a dull-yellow head and chest. Slightly smaller than the male.
Male:	black bird with a lemon-yellow head, breast and nape of neck, black mask, gray bill and white wing patches
Juvenile:	similar to female
Nest:	cup; female builds; 2 broods per year
Eggs:	3–5; greenish white with brown markings
Incubation:	11–13 days; female incubates
Fledging:	9–12 days; female feeds the young
Migration:	complete, to southern states and Mexico
Food:	insects, seeds; will come to ground feeders
Compare:	Female Red-winged Blackbird (p. 153) is smaller and has white eyebrows and heavy streaking. Look for the dull-yellow head to help identify the female Yellow-headed.

Stan's Notes: Found around marshes, wetlands and lakes. Nests in deep water, unlike its cousin, the Red-winged Blackbird, which prefers shallow water. Usually heard before seen. Gives a raspy, low, metallic-sounding call. The male is the only large black bird with a bright-yellow head. He gives an impressive mating display, flying with his head drooped and feet and tail pointing down while steadily beating his wings. Young keep low and out of sight for up to three weeks before they start to fly. Migrates in large flocks of as many as 200 birds, often with Red-winged Blackbirds and Brown-headed Cowbirds. Flocks of mainly males return in late March and early April; females return later. Most colonies consist of 20–100 nests.

Lesser Yellowlegs
Tringa flavipes

Size: 10–12" (25–30 cm)

Male: A typical sandpiper-type bird with a brown back and wings. Streaked white chest. Thin, straight black bill. Long yellow legs.

Female: same as male

Juvenile: same as adults

Nest: ground; female builds; 1 brood per year

Eggs: 3–4; yellowish with brown markings

Incubation: 22–23 days; male and female incubate

Fledging: 18–20 days; male and female lead the young to food

Migration: complete, to South America

Food: aquatic insects, tiny fish

Compare: The Greater Yellowlegs (p. 179) is much larger and has a longer, slightly upturned bill. Breeding Willet (p. 181) is larger and has brown legs. The breeding Spotted Sandpiper (p. 149) has black spots on its chest.

Stan's Notes: Usually seen in large flocks, combing shorelines and mudflats in search of aquatic insects. Usually walks with its head down and tail up, ready to snatch up prey. Uses its long, straight bill to pluck insects and tiny fish out of the water. A member of the sandpiper group known as Tattlers, which scream alarm calls when taking off. Quite often moves into the water before taking flight and gives a variety of flight notes at takeoff. Nest is a simple depression atop a mound of earth. Nests in marshes in the spruce forests of central Alaska and Canada. The nest is a simple depression atop a mound of earth.

Killdeer
Charadrius vociferus

SUMMER

Size: 11" (28 cm)

Male: Upland shorebird with 2 black bands around the neck, like a necklace. Brown back and white belly. Bright reddish-orange rump, visible in flight.

Female: same as male

Juvenile: similar to adults, with a single neck band

Nest: ground; male scrapes; 2 broods per year

Eggs: 3–5; tan with brown markings

Incubation: 24–28 days; male and female incubate

Fledging: 25 days; male and female lead their young to food

Migration: complete, to southern states, Mexico and Central America

Food: insects, worms, snails

Compare: The Spotted Sandpiper (p. 149) is found around water but lacks the 2 neck bands of the Killdeer.

Stan's Notes: Technically classified as a shorebird but lives in dry habitats instead of the shore. Often found in vacant fields, gravel pits, driveways, wetland edges or along railroad tracks. The only shorebird that has two black neck bands. Known to fake a broken wing to draw intruders away from the nest; once the nest is safe, the parent will take flight. Nests are just a slight depression in a dry area and are often hard to see. Hatchlings look like miniature adults walking on stilts. Soon after hatching, the young follow their parents around and peck for insects. Gives a loud and distinctive "kill-deer" call. Migrates in small flocks.

Brown Thrasher

Toxostoma rufum

Size: 11" (28 cm)

Male: Rust-red with a long tail. Heavy streaking on the breast and belly. Two white wing bars. Long, curved bill and bright-yellow eyes.

Female: same as male

Juvenile: same as adults but with grayish eyes

Nest: cup; female and male build; 2 broods per year

Eggs: 4–5; pale blue with brown markings

Incubation: 11–14 days; female and male incubate

Fledging: 10–13 days; female and male feed the young

Migration: complete, to southern states

Food: insects, fruit

Compare: American Robin (p. 253) and Gray Catbird (p. 245) are similar, but both are smaller and lack a streaked chest, rusty color and yellow eyes. Look for the long rusty-red tail to help identify the Brown Thrasher.

Stan's Notes: A prodigious songster. Sings along forest edges and in suburban yards. Often found in thick shrubs, where it will sing deliberate musical phrases, repeating each twice. The male Brown Thrasher has the largest documented repertoire of all North American songbirds, with more than 1,100 types of songs. Builds nest low in dense shrubs, often in fencerows. Quickly flies or runs on the ground in and out of thick shrubs. A noisy feeder due to its habit of turning over leaves, small rocks and branches to find food. This bird is more abundant in the central Great Plains than anywhere else in North America.

yellow-shafted male

yellow-shafted female

red-shafted male

red-shafted female

Northern Flicker
Colaptes auratus

YEAR-ROUND
SUMMER

Size: 12" (30 cm)

Male: Brown and black with a red or black mustache and black necklace. Speckled chest. Large white rump patch, seen only when flying.

Female: same as male but without a mustache

Juvenile: same as adult of the same sex

Nest: cavity; female and male excavate; 1 brood per year

Eggs: 5–8; white without markings

Incubation: 11–14 days; female and male incubate

Fledging: 25–28 days; female and male feed the young

Migration: complete, to southern states; non-migrator in South Dakota and parts of North Dakota

Food: insects (especially ants and beetles); comes to suet feeders

Compare: Flickers are the only brown-backed woodpeckers in the Dakotas.

Stan's Notes: This is the only woodpecker to regularly feed on the ground. Prefers ants and beetles and produces an antacid saliva that neutralizes the acidic defense of ants. Can be attracted to your yard with a nest box stuffed with sawdust. Yellow-shafted variety has golden-yellow wing linings and tails. Red-shafteds are winter visitors in North Dakota and year-round residents in South Dakota. Male yellow-shafteds have black mustaches; male red-shafteds have red mustaches. Where ranges of these varieties overlap in South Dakota, hybrids occur with salmon-colored wing linings as a result. Often reuses an old nest. Undulates deeply during flight, flashing color under its wings and tail and calling "wacka-wacka" loudly. Populations swell in winter with northern migrants.

Mourning Dove
Zenaida macroura

YEAR-ROUND
SUMMER

Size: 12" (30 cm)

Male: Smooth and fawn-colored. Gray patch on the head. Iridescent pink and greenish blue on the neck. Black spot behind and below the eyes. Black spots on the wings and tail. Pointed, wedged tail; white edges seen in flight.

Female: similar to male, but lacks the pink-and-green iridescent neck feathers

Juvenile: spotted and streaked plumage

Nest: platform; female and male build; 2 broods per year

Eggs: 2; white without markings

Incubation: 13–14 days; male incubates during the day, female incubates at night

Fledging: 12–14 days; female and male feed the young

Migration: partial migrator to non-migrator; will move around to find food

Food: seeds; will visit seed and ground feeders

Compare: Eurasian Collared-Dove (p. 255) has a black collar on the nape of its neck. Rock Pigeon (p. 257) is larger and has a wide range of color combinations.

Stan's Notes: Name comes from its mournful cooing. A ground feeder, bobbing its head as it walks. One of the few birds to drink without lifting its head, like the Rock Pigeon (p. 257). The parents feed the young (squab) a regurgitated liquid called crop-milk for their first few days of life. Platform nest is flimsy and often falls apart in storms. During takeoff and in flight, wind rushes through the bird's wing feathers, creating a characteristic whistling sound.

Upland Sandpiper
Bartramia longicauda

Size: 12" (30 cm)

Male: Overall brown shorebird. Long yellow legs, a short, brown-tipped yellow bill and white belly. Appears to have a thin neck and small head in relationship to its body.

Female: same as male

Juvenile: similar to adult

Nest: ground; female and male construct; 1 brood per year

Eggs: 3–4; off-white with red markings

Incubation: 21–27 days; female and male incubate

Fledging: 30–31 days; female and male feed young

Migration: complete, to South America

Food: insects, seeds

Compare: Breeding Spotted Sandpiper (p. 149) is smaller, has shorter legs, black spots on a white breast and is found in very different habitats. The Spotted Sandpiper is almost always near water while the Upland is in grassy meadows and prairies.

Stan's Notes: A shorebird of the dry grassland that is aptly named. Often seen standing on fence posts or other perches in a prairie or grassland habitat. Frequently found in prairies and grasslands that were burned, where foraging for food is easier. A true indicator of high-quality prairie habitat, this shorebird returns to a more watery habitat after breeding and just before migrating. Frequently holds its wings open over its back for several seconds just after landing. Formerly known as Upland Plover. Was hunted in the late 1800s.

winter

breeding

Pied-billed Grebe

Podilymbus podiceps

Size: 12–14" (30–36 cm)

Male: Small and brown with a black chin and fluffy white patch beneath the tail. Black ring around a thick, chicken-like, ivory bill. Winter bill is brown and unmarked.

Female: same as male

Juvenile: paler than adults, with white spots and a gray chest, belly and bill

Nest: floating platform; female and male construct; 1 brood per year

Eggs: 5–7; bluish white without markings

Incubation: 22–24 days; female and male incubate

Fledging: 45–60 days; female and male feed the young

Migration: complete, to southern states, Mexico and Central America

Food: crayfish, aquatic insects, fish

Compare: Look for the white patch under the tail and the thick bill to help identify the Pied-billed.

Stan's Notes: This common summer resident is often seen diving for food. When disturbed, it slowly sinks like a submarine, quickly compressing its feathers, forcing the air out. Was called Hell-diver due to the length of time it can stay submerged. Able to surface far from where it went under. Well suited to life on water, with short wings, lobed toes, and legs set close to the rear of its body. Swims easily but moves awkwardly on land. Very sensitive to pollution. Builds nest on a floating mat in water. "Grebe" may originate from the Breton word *krib*, meaning "crest," referring to the crested head plumes of many grebes, especially during breeding season.

Greater Yellowlegs
Tringa melanoleuca

MIGRATION

Size:	13–15" (33–38 cm)
Male:	Tall with a bulbous head and a long, thin, slightly upturned bill. Gray streaking on the chest. White belly. Long yellow legs.
Female:	same as male
Juvenile:	same as adults
Nest:	ground; female builds; 1 brood per year
Eggs:	3–4; off-white with brown markings
Incubation:	22–23 days; female and male incubate
Fledging:	18–20 days; male and female feed the young
Migration:	complete, to southern states, Mexico, and Central and South America
Food:	small fish, aquatic insects
Compare:	The Lesser Yellowlegs (p. 165) is much smaller and has a shorter bill. The Killdeer (p. 167) has 2 black bands around its neck. The breeding Spotted Sandpiper (p. 149) has spots on its chest. Look for the long yellow legs and long bill to identify the Greater Yellowlegs.

Stan's Notes: A common shorebird, often seen during migration. Can be identified by its long legs, which enable it to wade in deep water, and its slightly upturned bill. Often seen resting on one leg. Rushes forward through the water to feed, plowing its bill or swinging it from side to side, catching small fish and insects. A skittish bird, it is quick to give an alarm call, causing flocks to take flight. Typically moves into the water before taking flight. Gives a variety of "flight" notes at takeoff. Nests on the ground close to water on the northern tundra of Labrador and Newfoundland.

breeding

winter
p. 261

displaying

Willet

Catoptrophorus semipalmatus

SUMMER MIGRATION

Size: 14–16" (36–40 cm)

Male: Brown breeding plumage with a white belly. Brown bill and legs. Distinctive black-and-white wing lining pattern, seen in flight or during display.

Female: same as male

Juvenile: similar to breeding adult, more tan in color

Nest: ground; female builds; 1 brood per year

Eggs: 3–5; olive-green with dark markings

Incubation: 24–28 days; male and female incubate

Fledging: 1–2 days; female and male feed young

Migration: complete, to southern coastal states, coastal Central and South America

Food: insects, small fish, crabs, worms, clams

Compare: Lesser Yellowlegs (p. 165) is smaller and has yellow legs. Look for Willet's distinctive black-and-white wing linings.

Stan's Notes: Common summer resident in the Dakotas, also seen during migration. It appears a rich, warm brown during the breeding season and rather plain gray during the winter, but it always has a striking black-and-white wing pattern when seen in flight. Uses its black-and-white wing patches to display to its mate. Named after the "pill-will-willet" call it gives during the breeding season. Gives a "kip-kip-kip" alarm call when it takes flight. Nests along the Gulf and East Coasts, in some western states and Canada.

Green-winged Teal
Anas crecca

SUMMER

Size: 14–15" (36–38 cm)

Male: Chestnut head with a dark-green patch outlined with white from the eyes to the nape of neck. Gray body and butter-yellow tail. Green patch on the wings (speculum), seen in flight.

Female: light-brown duck with black spots and a green speculum, small bill

Juvenile: same as female

Nest: ground; female builds; 1 brood per year

Eggs: 8–10; cream-white without markings

Incubation: 21–23 days; female incubates

Fledging: 32–34 days; female teaches the young to feed

Migration: complete, to southern states

Food: aquatic plants and insects

Compare: Male Wood Duck (p. 281) is more colorful than male Green-winged. Female Blue-winged Teal (p. 185) is similar in size, but it is slightly white at the base of its bill.

Stan's Notes: A common summer duck, and a year-round resident in southern parts of South Dakota. It is one of the smallest dabbling ducks, tipping forward in water to glean aquatic plants and insects from the bottom of shallow ponds. This behavior makes it vulnerable to ingesting spent lead shot, which can cause death. It walks well on land and will also feed in flooded fields and woodlands. Known for its fast and agile flight. Groups wheel and spin through the air in tight formation. The green wing patches are most obvious during flight.

male

female

Blue-winged Teal
Spatula discors

Size: 15–16" (38–41 cm)

Male: Small, plain-looking brown duck with black speckles and a large, crescent-shaped white mark at the base of the bill. Gray head. Black tail with a small white patch. Blue wing patch (speculum), best seen in flight.

Female: duller than male, with only slight white at the base of the bill; lacks a crescent mark on the face and a white patch on the tail

Juvenile: same as female

Nest: ground; female builds; 1 brood per year

Eggs: 8–11; creamy white

Incubation: 23–27 days; female incubates

Fledging: 35–44 days; female feeds the young

Migration: complete, to southern states, Mexico and Central America

Food: aquatic plants, seeds, aquatic insects

Compare: The female Mallard (p. 203) has an orange-and-black bill. The female Wood Duck (p. 193) has a crest. Female Green-winged Teal (p. 183) is similar in size but lacks white at base of bill. Look for the white facial mark to identify the male Blue-winged.

Stan's Notes: An early migrator in North and South Dakota. Most breeding birds here leave before more-northern ducks pass through in autumn. Constructs nest some distance from water. Female performs a distraction display to protect nest and young. Male leaves female near the end of incubation. Planting crops and cultivating to pond edges have caused a decline in population.

male p. 65

female

Lesser Scaup
Aythya affinis

SUMMER
MIGRATION

Size: 16–17" (40–43 cm)

Female: Overall brown duck with a dull-white patch at the base of a light-gray bill. Yellow eyes.

Male: white and gray; the chest and head appear nearly black but the head looks purple with green highlights in direct sun; yellow eyes

Juvenile: same as female

Nest: ground; female builds; 1 brood per year

Eggs: 8–14; olive-buff without markings

Incubation: 22–28 days; female incubates

Fledging: 45–50 days; female teaches young to feed

Migration: complete, to southern states, Mexico, Central America and northern South America

Food: aquatic plants and insects

Compare: The male Blue-winged Teal (p. 185) is slightly smaller and has a crescent-shaped white mark at the base of its bill. The female Wood Duck (p. 193) is larger with white around the eyes.

Stan's Notes: A summer resident in North Dakota. Seen in South Dakota during migration. A common diving duck. Submerges itself completely to feed on the bottom of lakes (unlike dabbling ducks, which only tip forward to reach the bottom). Note the bold white stripe under the wings when in flight. The male leaves the female when she starts incubating eggs. The quantity of eggs (clutch size) increases with the age of the female. This species has an interesting babysitting arrangement in which groups of young (crèches) are tended by one to three adult females.

male p. 67

female

Ring-necked Duck
Aythya collaris

Size: 16–19" (41–48 cm)

Female: Brown with a darker-brown back and crown and lighter-brown sides. Gray face. White eye-ring with a white line behind the eye. White ring around the bill. Peaked head.

Male: black head, chest and back; gray-to-white sides; blue bill with a bold white ring and a thinner ring at the base; peaked head

Juvenile: similar to female

Nest: ground; female builds; 1 brood per year

Eggs: 8–10; olive to brown without markings

Incubation: 26–27 days; female incubates

Fledging: 49–56 days; female teaches the young to feed

Migration: complete, to southern states and Mexico

Food: aquatic plants and insects

Compare: Female Lesser Scaup (p. 187) is similar in size. Look for the white ring around the bill to help identify the female Ring-necked Duck.

Stan's Notes: Often seen in larger freshwater lakes, usually in small flocks or just pairs. A diving duck, watch for it to dive underwater to forage for food. Springs up off the water to take flight. Has a distinctive tall, peaked head with a sloped forehead. Flattens its crown when diving. Male gives a quick series of grating barks and grunts. Female gives high-pitched peeps. Named "Ring-necked" for its cinnamon collar, which is nearly impossible to see in the field. Also called Ring-billed Duck due to the white ring on its bill.

displaying

non-displaying

Greater Prairie-Chicken

Tympanuchus cupido

Size: 17" (43 cm)

Male: A chicken-like brown bird. White barring throughout. Short, rounded tail, fans out for display. Orange-to-yellow patches (air sacs) on the sides of neck and bright orange-to-yellow eyebrows (combs) during display.

Female: similar to male, darker with a tan throat

Juvenile: similar to adults

Nest: ground; female builds; 1 brood per year

Eggs: 7–12; olive with brown markings

Incubation: 23–24 days; female incubates

Fledging: 7–10 days; female shows young what to eat

Migration: non-migrator; moves around to find food

Food: insects, seeds, fruit

Compare: Wild Turkey (p. 225) is much larger and darker and has a longer tail and neck.

Stan's Notes: Market hunting and intensive agricultural practices have nearly eliminated this bird from much of its historical range, but it's now recovering. The Dakotas are also home to Lesser Prairie-Chickens (not shown), which are slightly smaller and grayer overall. Many males perform a loud animated dance together in spring in shorter grassy areas called leks. They bow forward, inflating air sacs, fanning tails, stomping feet, and giving a low moan (like air blowing across the top of an open bottle). Females watch for males who perform the best, fly into the arena to mate, then go off to build a nest and lay eggs.

male
p. 281

female

Wood Duck

Aix sponsa

SUMMER MIGRATION

Size: 17–20" (43–51 cm)

Female: Small brown dabbling duck. Bright-white eye-ring and a not-so-obvious crest. Blue patch on wings (speculum), often hidden.

Male: highly ornamented, with a mostly green head and crest patterned with black and white; rusty chest, white belly and red eyes

Juvenile: similar to female

Nest: cavity; female lines an old woodpecker cavity or a nest box in a tree; 1 brood per year

Eggs: 10–15; creamy white without markings

Incubation: 28–36 days; female incubates

Fledging: 56–68 days; female teaches the young to feed

Migration: complete, to southern states

Food: aquatic insects, plants, seeds

Compare: The female Mallard (p. 203) and female Blue-winged Teal (p. 185) lack the eye-ring and crest. The female Northern Shoveler (p. 201) is larger and has a large spoon-shaped bill.

Stan's Notes: A common duck of quiet, shallow backwater ponds. Nearly went extinct around 1900 due to overhunting, but it's doing well now. Nests in a tree cavity or a nest box in a tree. Seen flying in forests or perching on high branches. Female takes off with a loud, squealing call and enters the nest cavity from full flight. Lays some eggs in a neighboring nest (egg dumping), resulting in more than 20 eggs in some clutches. Hatchlings stay in the nest for 24 hours, then jump from as high as 60 feet (18 m) to the ground or water to follow their mother. They never return to the nest.

male

female

American Wigeon
Anas americana

SUMMER
MIGRATION

Size: 18–20" (48 cm)

Male: Brown duck with a rounded head and obvious white cap. Deep-green patch starting behind the eyes and streaking down the neck. Long pointed tail. Short, black-tipped grayish bill. White belly and wing linings, seen in flight. Non-breeding lacks white cap and green patch.

Female: light brown with a pale-gray head, a short, black-tipped grayish bill, green wing patch (speculum) and dark eye spot; white belly and wing linings, seen in flight

Juvenile: similar to female

Nest: ground; female builds; 1 brood per year

Eggs: 7–12; white without markings

Incubation: 23–25 days; female incubates

Fledging: 37–48 days; female teaches the young to feed

Migration: complete, to Texas, other southern states

Food: aquatic plants, seeds

Compare: Male American Wigeon is easily identified by the white cap and black-tipped grayish bill. Look for the black-tipped grayish bill and green wing patch to help identify the female American Wigeon.

Stan's Notes: Often in small flocks or with other ducks. Prefers shallow lakes. Male stays with the female only during the first week of incubation. Female raises the young. If threatened, female feigns injury while the young run and hide. Conceals nest in tall vegetation within 50–250 yards (46–229 m) of water.

male
p. 71

female

Common Goldeneye
Bucephala clangula

SUMMER
MIGRATION
WINTER

Size: 18–20" (45–51 cm)

Female: Brown and gray duck with a large dark-brown head and gray body. White collar. Bright-golden eyes. Yellow-tipped dark bill.

Male: mostly white with a black back, a puffy green head, a large white spot on the face, bright-golden eyes and a dark bill

Juvenile: same as female but with a dark bill

Nest: cavity; female lines an old woodpecker cavity; 1 brood per year

Eggs: 8–10; light green without markings

Incubation: 28–32 days; female incubates

Fledging: 56–59 days; female leads the young to food

Migration: complete, to southern states and Mexico; winters in parts of the Dakotas

Food: aquatic plants, insects, fish, mollusks

Compare: Similar to, but larger than, the brown and white female Lesser Scaup (p. 187). Look for the dark-brown head, white collar and golden-yellow eyes to help identify the female Common Goldeneye.

Stan's Notes: Known for the loud whistling sound produced by its wings during flight. During late winter and early spring, the male performs elaborate mating displays that include throwing his head back and calling a raspy note. Female will lay some of her eggs in other goldeneye nests or in the nests of other species (egg dumping), causing some mothers to incubate as many as 30 eggs in a brood. Named for its bright-golden eyes. Winters in the Dakotas wherever it can find open water.

male
p. 271

female

Gadwall
Mareca strepera

SUMMER

Size: 19" (48 cm)

Female: Mottled brown with a pronounced color change from dark-brown body to light-brown neck and head. Bright-white wing linings, seen in flight. Small white wing patch, seen when swimming. Gray bill with orange sides.

Male: plump gray duck with a brown head and distinctive black rump, white belly, bright-white wing linings, small white wing patch, chestnut-tinged wings, gray bill

Juvenile: similar to female

Nest: ground; female lines the nest with fine grass and down feathers plucked from her chest; 1 brood per year

Eggs: 8–11; white without markings

Incubation: 24–27 days; female incubates

Fledging: 48–56 days; young feed themselves

Migration: complete, to southern states and Mexico

Food: aquatic insects

Compare: Female Mallard (p. 203) is similar but has a blue-and-white wing mark. Look for Gadwall's white wing patch and gray bill with orange sides.

Stan's Notes: A duck of shallow marshes. Consumes mostly plant material, dunking its head in water to feed rather than tipping forward, like other dabbling ducks. Walks well on land; feeds in fields and woodlands. Nests within 300 feet (90 m) of water. Often in pairs with other duck species. Establishes pair bond during winter.

male p. 285

female

SUMMER

Northern Shoveler
Spatula clypeata

Size:	19–21" (48–53 cm)
Female:	A medium-sized brown duck speckled with black. Green patch on the wings (speculum). An extraordinarily large, spoon-shaped bill.
Male:	iridescent green head, rusty sides, white chest and a large spoon-shaped bill
Juvenile:	same as female
Nest:	ground; female builds; 1 brood per year
Eggs:	9–12; olive without markings
Incubation:	22–25 days; female incubates
Fledging:	30–60 days; female leads the young to food
Migration:	complete, to southern states, Mexico and Central America
Food:	aquatic insects, plants
Compare:	Female Mallard (p. 203) is similar but lacks the Shoveler's large bill. Female Wood Duck (p. 193) is smaller and has a white eye-ring. Look for Shoveler's large spoon-shaped bill to help identify.

Stan's Notes: One of several species of shovelers. Called "Shoveler" due to the peculiar, shovel-like shape of its bill. Given the common name "Northern" because it is the only species of these ducks in North America. Seen in shallow wetlands, ponds and small lakes in flocks of 5–10 birds. Flocks fly in tight formation. Swims low in water, pointing its large bill toward the water as if it's too heavy to lift. Usually swims in tight circles while feeding. Feeds mainly by filtering tiny aquatic insects and plants from the surface of the water with its bill.

201

female

male
p. 283

Mallard
Anas platyrhynchos

YEAR-ROUND
SUMMER

Size: 19–21" (48–53 cm)

Female: Brown duck with a blue-and-white wing mark (speculum). Orange-and-black bill.

Male: large green head, white necklace, rust-brown or chestnut chest, combination of gray-and-white sides, yellow bill, orange legs and feet

Juvenile: same as female but with a yellow bill

Nest: ground; female builds; 1 brood per year

Eggs: 7–10; greenish to whitish, unmarked

Incubation: 26–30 days; female incubates

Fledging: 42–52 days; female leads the young to food

Migration: non-migrator to partial in the Dakotas

Food: seeds, plants, aquatic insects; will come to ground feeders offering corn

Compare: Female Gadwall (p. 199) has a gray bill with orange sides. Female Northern Pintail (p. 205) is similar to female Mallard, but it has a gray bill. Female Northern Shoveler (p. 201) has a spoon-shaped bill. Female Wood Duck (p. 193) has a white eye-ring.

Stan's Notes: A familiar dabbling duck of lakes and ponds. Also found in rivers, streams and some backyards. Tips forward to feed on vegetation on the bottom of shallow water. The name "Mallard" comes from the Latin word *masculus,* meaning "male," referring to the male's habit of taking no part in raising the young. Female and male have white underwings and white tails, but only the male has black central tail feathers that curl upward. The female gives a classic quack. Returns to its birthplace each year.

Northern Pintail
Anas acuta

SUMMER

Size: 20" (52 cm), female
25" (63 cm), male

Male: A slender, elegant duck with a brown head, white neck and gray body. Gray bill. Extremely long and narrow black tail. Non-breeding has a pale-brown head that lacks the clear demarcation between the brown head and white neck. Lacks long tail feathers.

Female: mottled brown body with a paler head and neck, long tail, gray bill

Juvenile: similar to female

Nest: ground; female builds; 1 brood per year

Eggs: 6–9; olive-green without markings

Incubation: 22–25 days; female incubates

Fledging: 36–50 days; female teaches young to feed

Migration: complete, to southern states and Mexico

Food: aquatic plants and insects, seeds

Compare: The male Northern Pintail has a distinctive brown head and white neck and unique long tail feathers. Female Mallard (p. 203) is similar to female Pintail, but Mallard has an orange bill with black spots.

Stan's Notes: A common dabbling duck of alkaline marshes. About 90 percent of its diet is aquatic plants, except when females feed heavily on aquatic insects prior to nesting, presumably to gain extra nutrients for egg production. Male holds tail upright from the water's surface. No other North American duck has such a long tail.

male
p. 269

female

soaring

Northern Harrier

Circus hudsonius

YEAR-ROUND
SUMMER

Size: 18–22" (45–56 cm); up to 4' wingspan

Female: Slender, low-flying hawk with a dark-brown back and brown streaking on the chest and belly. Large white rump patch. Thin black tail bands and black wing tips. Yellow eyes.

Male: silver-gray with a large white rump patch and white belly, black wing tips, yellow eyes, faint, thin bands across the tail

Juvenile: similar to female, with an orange breast

Nest: ground; female and male construct; 1 brood per year

Eggs: 4–8; bluish white without markings

Incubation: 31–32 days; female incubates

Fledging: 30–35 days; male and female feed the young

Migration: partial migrator, to southern states, Mexico, and Central America; non-migrator in parts of South Dakota

Food: mice, snakes, insects, small birds

Compare: Slimmer than the Red-tailed Hawk (p. 211). Look for the characteristic low gliding and the black tail bands to identify the female Harrier.

Stan's Notes: One of the easiest of hawks to identify. Glides just above the ground, following the contours of the land while searching for prey. Holds its wings just above horizontal, tilting back and forth in the wind, similar to the Turkey Vulture. Formerly called Marsh Hawk due to its habit of hunting over marshes. Feeds and nests on the ground. Will also preen and rest on the ground. Unlike other hawks, mainly uses its hearing to find prey, followed by its sight. At any age, it has a distinctive owl-like face disk.

207

soaring light morph

intermediate morph

light morph

dark morph

soaring dark morph

Swainson's Hawk

Buteo swainsoni

Size: 19–22" (48–56 cm); up to 4¾' wingspan

Male: Highly variable plumage with three easily distinguishable color morphs. Light morph is brown and has a white belly, warm rusty chest and white face. Intermediate has a dark chest, rusty belly and white at the base of bill. Dark morph is nearly all dark brown with a rusty color low on the belly.

Female: same as male

Juvenile: similar to adult

Nest: platform; female and male construct; 1 brood per year

Eggs: 2–4; bluish or white with some brown marks

Incubation: 28–35 days; female and male incubate

Fledging: 28–30 days; female and male feed young

Migration: complete, to Central and South America

Food: small mammals, insects, snakes, birds

Compare: Slimmer than Red-tailed Hawk (p. 211), which has a white chest and brown belly band. Swainson's Hawk has longer, more pointed wings and a longer tail. Ferruginous Hawk (p. 215) lacks two-toned undersides of wings.

Stan's Notes: A slender open country hawk that hunts mammals, insects, snakes and birds when soaring (kiting) or perching. Often flies with slightly upturned wings in a teetering, vulture-like flight. The light morph is the most common, but the intermediate and dark are also common. Even minor nest disturbance can cause nest failure. Often gathers in large flocks to migrate.

soaring

juvenile
soaring

juvenile

Red-tailed Hawk

Buteo jamaicensis

YEAR-ROUND
SUMMER

Size: 19–23" (48–63 cm); up to 4½' wingspan

Male: Variety of colorations, from chocolate brown to nearly all white. Often brown with a white breast and brown belly band. Rust-red tail. Underside of wing is white with a small dark patch on the leading edge near the shoulder.

Female: same as male but slightly larger

Juvenile: similar to adults, with a speckled breast and light eyes; lacks a red tail

Nest: platform; male and female build; 1 brood per year

Eggs: 2–3; white without markings or sometimes marked with brown

Incubation: 30–35 days; female and male incubate

Fledging: 45–46 days; male and female feed the young

Migration: non-migrator to partial migrator

Food: small and medium-sized animals, large birds, snakes, fish, insects, bats, carrion

Compare: Swainson's Hawk (p. 209) is slimmer with longer, more pointed wings.

Stan's Notes: Common in open country and cities. Seen perching on fences, freeway lampposts and trees. Look for it circling above open fields and roadsides, searching for prey. Gives a high-pitched scream that trails off. Often builds a large stick nest in large trees along roads. Lines nest with finer material, like evergreen needles. Returns to the same nest site each year. The red tail develops in the second year and is best seen from above.

Great Horned Owl
Bubo virginianus

YEAR-ROUND

Size: 21–25" (53–64 cm); up to 4' wingspan

Male: Robust brown "horned" owl. Bright-yellow eyes and a V-shaped white throat resembling a necklace. Horizontal barring on the chest.

Female: same as male but slightly larger

Juvenile: similar to adults but lacks ear tufts

Nest: no nest; takes over the nest of a crow, hawk or Great Blue Heron or uses a partial cavity, stump or broken tree; 1 brood per year

Eggs: 2–3; white without markings

Incubation: 26–30 days; female incubates

Fledging: 30–35 days; male and female feed the young

Migration: non-migrator

Food: mammals, birds (ducks), snakes, insects

Compare: Burrowing Owl (p. 159) is much smaller and has long legs. Look for bright-yellow eyes and feather "horns" on the head to help identify the Great Horned Owl.

Stan's Notes: The largest resident owl in the state. One of the earliest nesters in the Dakotas, laying eggs in January and February. Able to hunt in complete darkness due to its excellent hearing. The "horns," or "ears," are tufts of feathers and have nothing to do with hearing. Cannot turn its head all the way around. Wing feathers are ragged on the ends, resulting in silent flight. Eyelids close from the top down, like humans. Fearless, it is one of the few animals that will kill skunks and porcupines. Given that, it is also called the Flying Tiger. Call sounds like "hoo-hoo-hoo-hoooo."

soaring

soaring
juvenile

juvenile

Ferruginous Hawk
Buteo regalis

Size: 22–26" (56–66 cm); up to 4' wingspan

Male: Pale-brown head, gray cheeks, and reddish back. White chin, chest and belly. Rust flanks extend down feathered legs. Bright-white undersides of wings. Light-rust wing linings. Tail white below, rust-tinged on top. Large, strong yellow feet. Red eyes. Dark eye line.

Female: same as male, but noticeably larger

Juvenile: brown head, nape, back and wings with a white chin, chest and belly

Nest: massive platform, low in a tree, sometimes on the ground; female and male construct; 1 brood per year

Eggs: 2–4; bluish or white, can have brown marks

Incubation: 28–33 days; female and male incubate

Fledging: 44–48 days; female and male feed young

Migration: partial to complete, to southwestern states, Mexico; some don't migrate in South Dakota

Food: larger mammals, snakes, insects, birds

Compare: Swainson's Hawk (p. 209) is smaller and has a dark trailing edge of wings. Red-tailed Hawk (p. 211) has a brown belly band and lacks rust flanks and legs.

Stan's Notes: The largest hawk species. Found in western prairies. Common name means "iron-like," referring to the rusty color. Male and female perform aerial courtships, soaring with wings held above their backs, male diving at female, grabbing each other with large, powerful feet. Often hunts larger mammals such as jackrabbits. Often stands on the ground. Nests in most of the Dakotas.

American Bittern
Botaurus lentiginosus

SUMMER

Size: 28" (71 cm)

Male: Overall brown with thick rusty striping on neck, chest and belly. White chin. A unique shape with an extremely long neck, round compact body and short tail. Green legs and feet. Long, pointed yellow bill. Golden eyes.

Female: same as male

Juvenile: similar to adult

Nest: ground; female builds; 1 brood per year

Eggs: 4–5; light brown without markings

Incubation: 28–29 days; female incubates

Fledging: 7–14 days; male and female teach young what to eat

Migration: complete, to southern coastal states, Mexico

Food: small fish, aquatic insects, amphibians

Compare: The Black-crowned Night-Heron (p. 77) is gray and white with a black cap and dark bill. Great Blue Heron (p. 275) is much larger and has grayish-blue plumage.

Stan's Notes: Very secretive bird that seems to be on the decline. Hunts by walking extremely slowly, looking for prey along edges of ponds, streams and wetlands. Strikes an erect posture and points its large yellow bill straight up into the air to disguise itself. Carries this camouflage one step further, swaying back and forth in wind to match surrounding cattails and other aquatic vegetation (reeds). Strikes quickly at prey with its sharp bill. Usually solitary, roosting in trees at any hour. The male's loud booming call sounds like a slow water pump, hence its other common name, Slough-pumper.

in flight

Greater White-fronted Goose
Anser albifrons

MIGRATION

Size: 28" (71 cm); up to 4½' wingspan

Male: Grayish-brown bird with a distinctive white band at base of bill. Irregular black barring on the breast and belly. Bill is light pink to orange. Orange legs and feet. White rump and undertail.

Female: same as male

Juvenile: lighter color than adult and has yellowish legs, feet and bill

Nest: ground; female builds; 1 brood per year

Eggs: 4–7; creamy white without markings

Incubation: 23–25 days; female incubates

Fledging: 40–45 days; male and female teach young to feed

Migration: complete, to coastal Texas and Mexico

Food: aquatic plants and insects

Compare: Similar size as the Snow Goose (p. 309). White morph Snow Goose is all white with black wing tips and a large, bright pink bill. Blue morph Snow Goose often has a white head and dark-gray body.

Stan's Notes: Over half of the North American population (over 1 million birds) migrate through the Dakotas. Hybridizes with Snow and Canada Geese; often seen with them in mixed flocks or flying high up in large wedge shapes. Learns migratory route from parents and older members of flock. Doesn't breed until 3 years of age. Nests in Canadian Northwest Territories and Alaska. Often called Speckle-belly by hunters due to the irregular marking on belly.

Ring-necked Pheasant
Phasianus colchicus

YEAR-ROUND

Size: 30–36" (76–91 cm), male, including tail
21–25" (53–64 cm), female, including tail

Male: Golden-brown body with a long tail. White ring around the neck. Head is purple, green, blue and red.

Female: smaller and less flamboyant than the male, with brown plumage and a long tail

Juvenile: similar to female, with a shorter tail

Nest: ground; female builds; 1 brood per year

Eggs: 8–10; olive-brown without markings

Incubation: 23–25 days; female incubates

Fledging: 11–12 days; female leads the young to food

Migration: non-migrator

Food: insects, seeds, fruit; visits ground feeders

Compare: Male and female Pheasants have long tails, but the male is brightly colored.

Stan's Notes: Originally introduced to North America from China in the late 1800s. Common now throughout the U.S. Like many other game birds, its numbers vary greatly, making it common in some years, scarce in others. Seeks shelter during harsh winter weather. To attract females, the male gives a cackling call and then rapidly flutters his wings. Takes off in an explosive flight with fast wingbeats followed by gliding low to the ground. The name "Ring-necked" refers to the white ring around the male's neck. "Pheasant" comes from the Greek word *phaisianos*, which means "bird of the River Phasis" (known today as the Rioni River).

soaring

juvenile

juvenile

Golden Eagle
Aquila chrysaetos

YEAR-ROUND
MIGRATION
WINTER

Size: 30–40" (76–102 cm); up to 7¼' wingspan

Male: Uniform dark brown with a golden-yellow head and nape of neck. Yellow around base of bill. Yellow feet.

Female: same as male

Juvenile: similar to adult, with white "wrist" patches and a white base of tail

Nest: platform, on a cliff; female and male build; 1 brood per year

Eggs: 1–2; white with brown markings

Incubation: 43–45 days; female and male incubate

Fledging: 63–75 days; female and male feed young

Migration: partial migrator to non-migrator; moves around to find food in winter

Food: mammals, birds, reptiles, insects

Compare: The Bald Eagle (p. 81) adult is similar, but it has a white head and white tail. Bald Eagle juvenile is often confused with the Golden Eagle juvenile; both are large dark birds with white markings.

Stan's Notes: A large, powerful raptor that has no trouble taking larger prey such as jackrabbits. Hunts by perching or soaring and watching for movement. Inhabits open terrain, requiring large territories to provide a large supply of food. Long-term pair bond, renewing its bond late in winter with spectacular high-flying courtship displays. Usually nests on cliff faces; rarely nests in trees. Uses a well-established nest that's been used for generations. Will add items to the nest such as antlers, bones and barbed wire.

223

displaying male

non-displaying

female

Wild Turkey
Meleagris gallopavo

YEAR-ROUND

Size: 36–48" (91–122 cm)

Male: Large brown-and-bronze bird with a naked blue-and-red head. Long, straight, black beard in the center of the chest. Tail spreads open like a fan. Spurs on legs.

Female: thinner and less striking than the male; often lacks a breast beard

Juvenile: same as adult of the same sex

Nest: ground; female builds; 1 brood per year

Eggs: 10–12; buff-white with dull-brown markings

Incubation: 27–28 days; female incubates

Fledging: 6–10 days; female leads the young to food

Migration: non-migrator; moves around to find food

Food: insects, seeds, fruit

Compare: This bird is quite distinctive and unlikely to be confused with others.

Stan's Notes: The largest game bird in the Dakotas, and the species from which the domestic turkey was bred. A strong flier that can approach 60 miles (97 km) per hour. Can fly straight up, then away. Eyesight is three times better than ours. Hearing is also excellent; can hear competing males up to a mile away. Male has a "harem" of up to 20 females. Female scrapes out a shallow depression for nesting and pads it with soft leaves. Males are known as toms, females are hens, and young are poults. Roosts in trees at night. Nearly eliminated from the Dakotas by the turn of the twentieth century due to market hunting and loss of habitat. Restoration efforts began in the 1950s and continue today. Populations are now stable.

Ruby-crowned Kinglet
Regulus calendula

Size: 4" (10 cm)

Male: Small, teardrop-shaped green-to-gray bird. Two white wing bars and a white eye-ring. Hidden ruby crown.

Female: same as male, but lacks a ruby crown

Juvenile: same as female

Nest: pendulous; female builds; 1 brood per year

Eggs: 4–5; white with brown markings

Incubation: 11–12 days; female incubates

Fledging: 11–12 days; female and male feed the young

Migration: complete, to southern states, Mexico and Central America

Food: insects, berries

Compare: The female American Goldfinch (p. 317) shares the drab olive plumage and unmarked chest, but it is larger. Look for the white eye-ring to identify the Ruby-crowned Kinglet.

Stan's Notes: This is one of the smaller birds in the Dakotas. Usually seen only during migration, except in the Black Hills of South Dakota. Look for it flitting around thick shrubs low to the ground. It takes a quick eye to see the ruby crown, which the male flashes when he is excited. The female weaves an unusually intricate nest and fastens colorful lichens and mosses to the exterior with spiderwebs. Often builds the nest high in a mature tree, where it hangs from a branch that has overlapping leaves. Sings a distinctive song that starts out soft and ends loud and on a higher note. "Kinglet" originates from the word *king*, referring to the male's red crown, and the diminutive suffix *let*, meaning "small."

Red-breasted Nuthatch
Sitta canadensis

YEAR-ROUND
WINTER

Size: 4½" (11 cm)

Male: Gray-backed bird with an obvious black eye line and black cap. Rust-red breast and belly.

Female: duller than male and has a gray cap and pale undersides

Juvenile: same as female

Nest: cavity; male and female excavate a cavity or move into a vacant hole; 1 brood per year

Eggs: 5–6; white with red-brown markings

Incubation: 11–12 days; female incubates

Fledging: 14–20 days; female and male feed the young

Migration: irruptive; moves around North and South Dakota in search of food in winter

Food: insects, insect eggs, seeds; comes to seed and suet feeders

Compare: White-breasted Nuthatch (p. 235) is larger and does not have the rust-red breast and black eye line of Red-breasted Nuthatch.

Stan's Notes: The nuthatch climbs down trunks of trees headfirst, searching for insects. Like a chickadee, it grabs a seed from a feeder and flies off to crack it open. It wedges the seed into a crevice and pounds it open with several sharp blows. The name "Nuthatch" comes from the Middle English moniker *nuthak,* referring to the habit of hacking seeds open. Look for it in mature conifers, where it extracts seeds from pine cones. Excavates a cavity or takes an old woodpecker hole or a natural cavity and builds a nest within. Gives a series of nasal "yank-yank-yank" calls. A winter visitor and a year-round resident in some parts of North and South Dakota. More abundant in some years and absent in others.

Black-capped Chickadee

Poecile atricapillus

YEAR-ROUND

Size: 5" (13 cm)

Male: Familiar gray bird with a black cap and throat patch. Tan sides and belly. White chest. Small white wing marks.

Female: same as male

Juvenile: same as adult

Nest: cavity; female and male excavate or use a nest box; 1 brood per year

Eggs: 5–7; white with fine brown markings

Incubation: 11–13 days; female and male incubate

Fledging: 14–18 days; female and male feed the young

Migration: non-migrator

Food: insects, seeds, fruit; comes to seed and suet feeders

Compare: A familiar backyard bird whose energy and friendliness are hard to mistake.

Stan's Notes: Widespread, common bird throughout the Dakotas. A perky backyard bird that can be attracted with a nest box or bird feeder. Usually the first to find a new seed or suet feeder. Can be easily tamed and hand-fed. Much of the diet comes from bird feeders, so it can be a common urban bird. Needs to feed every day in winter, and forages to find food even during the worst winter storms. Typically seen with nuthatches, woodpeckers and other birds. Builds nest mostly with green moss and lines it with fur. Named "Chickadee" for its familiar "chika-dee-dee-dee-dee" call. Also gives a high-pitched, two-toned "fee-bee" call. Can have different calls in different regions.

female
p. 113

male

Dark-eyed Junco
Junco hyemalis

WINTER

Size: 5½" (14 cm)

Male: Plump, dark-eyed bird with a slate-gray-to-charcoal chest, head and back. White belly. Pink bill. White outer tail feathers appear like a white V in flight.

Female: round with brown plumage

Juvenile: similar to female, with streaking on the breast and head

Nest: cup; female and male build; 2 broods per year

Eggs: 3–5; white with reddish-brown markings

Incubation: 12–13 days; female incubates

Fledging: 10–13 days; male and female feed the young

Migration: complete, throughout the U.S.; winters in the Dakotas

Food: seeds, insects; visits ground and seed feeders

Compare: Rarely confused with any other bird. Look for the pink bill and small flocks feeding under feeders to identify the male Dark-eyed Junco.

Stan's Notes: Common in winter, this bird is usually seen on the ground in small flocks. Adheres to a rigid social hierarchy, with dominant birds chasing the less dominant birds. Look for the white outer tail feathers flashing in flight. Most comfortable on the ground, juncos will us their feet to simultaneously "double-scratch" to expose seeds and insects. Eats many weed seeds. Several sub-species of Dark-eyed Junco were previously considered to be separate species but have now been combined into one. Doesn't nest in the Dakotas.

White-breasted Nuthatch
Sitta carolinensis

YEAR-ROUND

Size: 5–6" (13–15 cm)

Male: Slate gray with a white face, breast and belly. Large white patch on the rump. Black cap and nape. Bill is long and thin, slightly upturned. Chestnut undertail.

Female: similar to male, but has a gray cap and nape

Juvenile: similar to female

Nest: cavity; female and male build a nest within; 1 brood per year

Eggs: 5–7; white with brown markings

Incubation: 11–12 days; female incubates

Fledging: 13–14 days; female and male feed the young

Migration: non-migrator

Food: insects, insect eggs, seeds; comes to seed and suet feeders

Compare: Red-breasted Nuthatch (p. 229) is smaller and has a rust-red belly and distinctive black eye line.

Stan's Notes: The nuthatch hops headfirst down trees, looking for insects missed by birds climbing up. Its climbing agility is due to an extra-long hind toe claw, or nail, that is nearly twice the size of its front claws. "Nuthatch," from the Middle English *nuthak*, refers to the bird's habit of wedging a seed in a crevice and hacking it open. Often seen in flocks with chickadees and Downy Woodpeckers. Mates stay together year-round, defending a small territory. Gives a characteristic "whi-whi-whi-whi" spring call during February and March. One of nearly 30 worldwide nuthatch species.

male

first winter

female

Yellow-rumped Warbler

Setophaga coronata

SUMMER MIGRATION

Size: 5–6" (13–15 cm)

Male: Slate gray with black streaking on the chest. Yellow patches on the head, flanks and rump. White chin and belly. Two white wing bars.

Female: duller gray than the male, mixed with brown

Juvenile: first winter is similar to the adult female

Nest: cup; female builds; 2 broods per year

Eggs: 4–5; white with brown markings

Incubation: 12–13 days; female incubates

Fledging: 10–12 days; female and male feed young

Migration: complete, to southern states, Mexico and Central America

Food: insects, berries; visits suet feeders in spring

Compare: The male Common Yellowthroat (p. 319) has a yellow chest and distinctive black mask. The male Yellow Warbler (p. 323) is all yellow with orange streaks on breast. Look for patches of yellow on the rump, head, flanks and chin of Yellow-rumped Warbler to help identify.

Stan's Notes: A common migrating warbler and summer resident in parts of the Dakotas. Flocks of hundreds seen during migration, usually arriving in late September to early October. Familiar call is a single robust "chip," heard mostly during migration. Sings a wonderful song in spring. Moves quickly among trees and from the ground to trees. Flits around the upper branches of tall trees. Builds nest in coniferous and aspen forests. In the fall, the male molts to a dull color similar to the female, but he retains his yellow patches all year. Frequently called Myrtle Warbler in eastern states and Audubon's Warbler in western states. Sometimes called Butter-butt due to the yellow patch on its rump.

Eastern Phoebe
Sayornis phoebe

SUMMER
MIGRATION

Size: 7" (18 cm)

Male: Plain gray with slightly darker wings and a light-olive belly. Thin, dark bill.

Female: same as male

Juvenile: same as adults

Nest: cup; female builds; 2 broods per year

Eggs: 4–5; white without markings

Incubation: 15–16 days; female incubates

Fledging: 15–16 days; male and female feed the young

Migration: complete, to southern states and Mexico

Food: insects

Compare: The Gray Catbird (p. 245) has a black crown and a chestnut patch under its tail. Eastern Phoebe lacks any distinctive markings. Listen for its well-enunciated "fee-bee" call and look for the hawking and tail-pumping behaviors to help identify this bird.

Stan's Notes: A sparrow-sized bird that often perches on the end of a dead branch. Found in forests, yards and farms. In a process called hawking, it waits for a passing insect. When a bug flies near, it launches out to catch it and then returns to the same branch. It has a distinctive habit of pumping its tail up and down while perching. Builds nest beneath the eaves of houses, under bridges or in other sheltered spots. Uses mud, grass and moss for nest materials and hair (and sometimes feathers) for the lining. The common name is derived from its distinct "fee-bee" call, which it repeats over and over from the top of dead branches.

Great Crested Flycatcher

Myiarchus crinitus

Size: 8" (20 cm)

Male: Gray head with a prominent crest. Gray back and throat. Yellow from the belly to the base of a reddish-brown tail. Lower bill is yellow at the base.

Female: same as male

Juvenile: same as adults

Nest: cavity; female and male stuff a vacant wood-pecker cavity or nest box; 1 brood per year

Eggs: 4–6; white to buff with brown markings

Incubation: 13–15 days; female incubates

Fledging: 14–21 days; female and male feed the young

Migration: complete, to Mexico and Central America

Food: insects, fruit

Compare: The Eastern Kingbird (p. 243) has a white band across its tail. The Eastern Phoebe (p. 239) is similar, but it lacks a crest and yellow belly. Look for the crest to identify the Flycatcher.

Stan's Notes: A common bird of wooded areas throughout North and South Dakota. It lives high up in trees, rarely coming to the ground. Makes long flights from treetop to treetop, moving from one hunting area to another. Gleans insects from tree leaves. Often heard before seen. "Great Crested" refers to the set of extra-long feathers on top of its head (crest), which the bird raises when alert or agitated, like the Northern Cardinal. Nests in an old woodpecker hole but can be attracted with a man-made nest box that has an entrance hole 1½–2½ inches (4–6 cm) in diameter. Often stuffs the cavity with a collection of fur, feathers, string and snake skins.

SUMMER

Eastern Kingbird
Tyrannus tyrannus

Size: 8" (20 cm)

Male: Mostly gray and black with a white chin and belly. Black head and tail with a distinct white band on the tip of the tail. Concealed red crown, rarely seen.

Female: same as male

Juvenile: same as adults

Nest: cup; male and female build; 1 brood per year

Eggs: 3–4; white with brown markings

Incubation: 16–18 days; female incubates

Fledging: 16–18 days; female and male feed the young

Migration: complete, to Mexico, Central America and South America

Food: insects, fruit

Compare: American Robin (p. 253) is larger and has a rust-red breast. Western Kingbird (p. 335) is yellow on the belly and under the wings. Look for the white band along the end of the tail to identify.

Stan's Notes: Common bird throughout the Dakotas in open fields and prairies. Autumn migration begins in late August and early September. As many as 20 birds migrate in a group. Returns to the mating ground in spring, where pairs defend their territory. Seems to be unafraid of other birds and chases larger birds. Given the common name "King" for its bold attitude and behavior. In a hunting technique known as hawking, it perches on a branch and watches for insects, flies out to catch one, and then returns to the same perch. Swoops from perch to perch when hunting. Becomes very vocal during late summer, when family members call back and forth to one another while hunting for insects.

Gray Catbird
Dumetella carolinensis

SUMMER

Size: 9" (23 cm)

Male: Handsome slate-gray bird with a black crown and a long, thin black bill. Often lifts up its tail, exposing a chestnut patch beneath.

Female: same as male

Juvenile: same as adults

Nest: cup; female and male build; 2 broods per year

Eggs: 4–6; blue-green without markings

Incubation: 12–13 days; female incubates

Fledging: 10–11 days; female and male feed the young

Migration: complete, to southern states

Food: insects, occasional fruit; visits suet feeders

Compare: The Eastern Phoebe (p. 239) is smaller and has an olive belly. The Eastern Kingbird (p. 243) is similar in size but has a white belly and a white band across its tail. To identify the Gray Catbird, look for the black crown and chestnut patch under the tail.

Stan's Notes: Returns to North and South Dakota by the last week of April. Seen in great numbers during fall migration in the last week of September and in early October. A secretive bird, more often heard than seen. The Chippewa Indians gave it a name that means "the bird that cries with grief" due to its raspy call. Called "Catbird" because the sound is like the meowing of a house cat. Often mimics other birds, rarely repeating the same phrases. Found in forest edges, backyards and parks. Builds its nest with small twigs. Nests in thick shrubs and quickly flies back into shrubs if approached. If a cowbird lays an egg in its nest, the catbird will quickly break it and eject it.

Loggerhead Shrike
Lanius ludovicianus

Size: 9" (22.5 cm)

Male: Gray head and back and a white chin, breast and belly. Black wings, tail, legs and feet. Black mask across the eyes and a black bill with a hooked tip. White wing patches, seen in flight.

Female: same as male

Juvenile: dull version of adult

Nest: cup; male and female construct; 1–2 broods per year

Eggs: 4–7; off-white with dark markings

Incubation: 16–17 days; female incubates

Fledging: 17–21 days; female and male feed the young

Migration: complete, to southern states and Mexico

Food: insects, lizards, small mammals, frogs

Compare: Distinctive-looking birds. Look for the black wings and mask across the eyes to help identify it. The Cedar Waxwing (p. 145) also has a black mask, but it is a brown bird, not gray and black like the Loggerhead Shrike.

Stan's Notes: The Loggerhead is a songbird that acts like a bird of prey. Known for skewering prey on barbed wire fences, thorns and other sharp objects to store or hold still while tearing apart to eat, hence its other common name, Butcher Bird. Feet are too weak to hold the prey it eats. Breeding bird surveys indicate declining populations in the Great Plains due to pesticides killing its major food source—grasshoppers.

red morph

gray morph

Eastern Screech-Owl

Megascops asio

Size: 8–10" (20–25 cm); up to 2' wingspan

Male: Small "eared" owl that occurs in different colorations. Gray morph is mottled gray and white. Red morph is mottled rust and white. Short wings. Bright-yellow eyes.

Female: same as male but slightly larger

Juvenile: lighter color than adults of the same morph and usually lacks ear tufts

Nest: cavity, old woodpecker cavity or man-made nest box; does not add any nesting material; 1 brood per year

Eggs: 4–5; white without markings

Incubation: 25–26 days; female incubates, male feeds the female during incubation

Fledging: 26–27 days; male and female feed the young

Migration: non-migrator; moves around in winter

Food: large insects, small mammals, birds, snakes

Compare: This is the only small owl in the Dakotas with ear tufts. Can be gray or rust in color.

Stan's Notes: Commonly found in forests that have suitable natural cavities for nesting and roosting. Active from dusk to dawn. Usually gives a tremulous, descending trill, like a sound effect in a scary movie. Seldom gives a screeching call. Often seen sunning itself at a nest-box hole during winter. Mates may have a long-term pair bond and may roost together at night. Excellent hearing and eyesight. Flaps rapidly and flies silently. Has winter and summer territories. The gray morph is more common than the red.

SUMMER

Wilson's Phalarope
Phalaropus tricolor

Size: 9½" (23 cm)

Female: An overall gray bird with a black stripe that runs from the base of bill across eyes and down the neck. Rusty wash on the front of neck. White chin and sides of body. Long black legs. Thin black bill.

Male: similar to female, but duller

Juvenile: similar to male, but has yellow legs

Nest: ground; male builds; 1–2 broods per year

Eggs: 3–4; pale white, brown and black markings

Incubation: 16–21 days; male incubates

Fledging: 8–10 days; male teaches young what to eat

Migration: complete, to South America

Food: small aquatic insects, seeds

Compare: Upland Sandpiper (p. 175) has a yellow bill. Breeding Spotted Sandpiper (p. 149) has a speckled white chest and belly. Lesser Yellowlegs (p. 165) lacks the female's neck stripe. Look for it swimming in tight circles.

Stan's Notes: Unique shorebird, one of the few that swims. Female is often larger and more colorful than male. Female abandons male after laying eggs. Male incubates eggs and cares for young. Often swims in tight circles, creating a whirlpool effect that raises insects to the surface. Picks insects off the water. Unlike other shorebirds, has lobed toes. Often seen alone or in small groups. Often feeds with American Avocets in shallow water. One of three phalarope species in North America and the only one that breeds south of Canada and Alaska. Breeding season from April to August.

American Robin
Turdus migratorius

YEAR-ROUND
SUMMER

Size: 9–11" (23–28 cm)

Male: Familiar gray bird with a dark rust-red breast and a nearly black head and tail. White chin with black streaks. White eye-ring.

Female: similar to male, with a duller rust-red breast and a gray head

Juvenile: similar to female, with a speckled breast and brown back

Nest: cup; female builds with help from the male; 2–3 broods per year

Eggs: 4–7; pale blue without markings

Incubation: 12–14 days; female incubates

Fledging: 14–16 days; female and male feed the young

Migration: complete, to southern states, Mexico and Central America; non-migrator in South Dakota and southern half of North Dakota

Food: insects, fruit, berries, earthworms

Compare: Familiar bird to all. To differentiate the male from the female, compare the nearly black head and rust-red chest of the male with the gray head and duller chest of the female.

Stan's Notes: Although complete migrators in northern states, the robin is a year-round resident in the southern half of North Dakota and throughout South Dakota. Can be heard singing all night long in spring. City robins sing louder than country robins in order to hear one another over traffic and noise. A robin isn't listening for worms when it turns its head to one side. It is focusing its sight out of one eye to look for dirt moving, which is caused by worms moving. Territorial, often fighting its reflection in a window.

253

Eurasian Collared-Dove
Streptopelia decaocto

YEAR-ROUND

Size: 12½" (32 cm)

Male: Head, neck, breast and belly are gray to tan. Back, wings and tail are slightly darker. Thin black collar with a white border on the nape of the neck. Tail is long and squared.

Female: same as male

Juvenile: similar to adults

Nest: platform; female and male build; 2–3 broods per year

Eggs: 3–5; creamy white without markings

Incubation: 12–14 days; female and male incubate

Fledging: 12–14 days; female and male feed the young

Migration: non-migrator

Food: seeds; will visit ground and seed feeders

Compare: The Mourning Dove (p. 173) is slightly smaller and darker. The Rock Pigeon (p. 257) has colorful iridescent patches. Look for the black collar on the nape and the squared tail to help identify the Eurasian Collared-Dove.

Stan's Notes: This non-native bird has spread into the Dakotas, having moved into Florida in the early 1980s after inadvertent introduction to the Bahamas. It has been expanding its range across North America and is predicted to spread just like it did through Europe from Asia. Unknown how this "new" bird will affect populations of the native Mourning Dove. Nearly identical to the Ringed Turtle-Dove, a common pet bird. The dark mark on the back of the neck gave rise to the common name. Look for flashes of white in the tail and dark wing tips when it lands or takes off.

YEAR-ROUND

Rock Pigeon
Columba livia

Size: 13" (33 cm)

Male: No set color pattern. Shades of gray to white with patches of gleaming, iridescent green and blue. Often has a light rump patch.

Female: same as male

Juvenile: same as adults

Nest: platform; female builds; 3–4 broods per year

Eggs: 1–2; white without markings

Incubation: 18–20 days; female and male incubate

Fledging: 25–26 days; female and male feed the young

Migration: non-migrator

Food: seeds

Compare: The Eurasian Collared-Dove (p. 255) has a black collar on the nape. The Mourning Dove (p. 173) is smaller and light brown and lacks the variety of color combinations of the Rock Pigeon.

Stan's Notes: Also known as the Domestic Pigeon. Formerly known as the Rock Dove. Introduced to North America from Europe by the early settlers. Most common around cities and barnyards, where it scratches for seeds. One of the few birds with a wide variety of colors, produced by years of selective breeding while in captivity. Parents feed the young a regurgitated liquid known as crop-milk for the first few days of life. One of the few birds that can drink without tilting its head back. Nests under bridges or on buildings, balconies, barns and sheds. Was once thought to be a nuisance in cities and was poisoned. Now, many cities have Peregrine Falcons (p. 267) feeding on Rock Pigeons, which keeps their numbers in check.

in flight

winter

breeding

Franklin's Gull

Leucophaeus pipixcan

Size: 14–15" (36–38 cm); up to 3' wingspan

Male: Gray-and-white gull with a black head and black extending partially down the front of neck. Black wing tips. Large white eye-ring. Reddish bill. Winter plumage has a partial black "hood" and a mostly black bill.

Female: same as male

Juvenile: brown back, partially black head, black bill

Nest: floating platform; male and female construct; 1 brood per year

Eggs: 2–4; greenish with brown markings

Incubation: 24–25 days; female and male incubate

Fledging: 31–33 days; female and male feed the young

Migration: complete, to southern states, Mexico, Central and South America

Food: insects, fish

Compare: The only black-headed gull in the Dakotas during summer and migration. Look for it in open marshes, with its black "hood" and black wing tips.

Stan's Notes: Usually seen during spring and autumn migrations, when hundreds gather in prairie lakes. A three-year gull. Juveniles have brown backs, partly black heads and black bills. First- and second-year birds look similar to winter adults, with gray-and-white plumage, partly black heads and black bills. Obtains adult plumage at three years. Winters on the Pacific Coast, all along Central and South America. Breeds in prairie pothole region.

breeding
p. 181

displaying

winter

Willet

Catoptrophorus semipalmatus

SUMMER
MIGRATION

Size: 14–16" (36–40 cm)

Male: Winter plumage is gray with a white belly. A distinctive black-and-white wing lining pattern, seen in flight or during display. Gray bill and legs.

Female: same as male

Juvenile: similar to breeding adult, more tan in color

Nest: ground; female builds; 1 brood per year

Eggs: 3–5; olive-green with dark markings

Incubation: 24–28 days; male and female incubate

Fledging: 1–2 days; female and male feed young

Migration: complete, to southern coastal states, coastal Central and South America

Food: insects, small fish, crabs, worms, clams

Compare: Larger than Lesser Yellowlegs (p. 165), which has yellow legs.

Stan's Notes: Common summer resident in the Dakotas, also seen during migration. It appears a rich, warm brown during the breeding season and rather plain gray during the winter, but it always has a striking black-and-white wing pattern when seen in flight. Uses its black-and-white wing patches to display to its mate. Named after the "pill-will-willet" call it gives during the breeding season. Gives a "kip-kip-kip" alarm call when it takes flight. Nests along the Gulf and East Coasts, in some western states and Canada.

soaring

juvenile

Sharp-shinned Hawk
Accipiter striatus

SUMMER
MIGRATION
WINTER

Size: 10–14" (25–36 cm); up to 2' wingspan

Male: Small woodland hawk with a gray back and head and a rust-red chest. Short wings. Long, squared tail and several dark tail bands, with the widest at the end of the tail. Red eyes.

Female: same as male but larger

Juvenile: same size as adults, with a brown back, heavy streaking on the chest and yellow eyes

Nest: platform; female builds; 1 brood per year

Eggs: 4–5; white with brown markings

Incubation: 32–35 days; female incubates

Fledging: 24–27 days; female and male feed the young

Migration: complete, to southern states, Mexico, Central America; winters in parts of South Dakota

Food: birds, small mammals

Compare: Cooper's Hawk (p. 265) is larger and has a larger head, a slightly longer neck and a rounded tail. Look for the squared tail to help identify the Sharp-shinned Hawk.

Stan's Notes: A hawk of backyards, parks and woodlands. Seen swooping on birds visiting feeders and chasing them as they flee. Its short wingspan and long tail help it to maneuver through thick stands of trees in pursuit of prey. Calls a loud, high-pitched "kik-kik-kik-kik." Named "Sharp-shinned" for the sharp projection (keel) on the leading edge of its shin. A bird's shin is actually below the ankle (rather than above it, like ours) on the tarsus bone of its foot. In most birds, the tarsus bone is rounded, not sharp.

soaring

juvenile

Cooper's Hawk
Accipiter cooperii

Size: 14–20" (36–51 cm); up to 3' wingspan

Male: Medium-sized hawk with short wings and a long, rounded tail with several black bands. Slate-gray back, rusty breast, dark wing tips. Gray bill with a bright-yellow spot at the base. Dark-red eyes.

Female: similar to male but larger

Juvenile: brown back, brown streaking on the breast, bright-yellow eyes

Nest: platform; male and female construct; 1 brood per year

Eggs: 2–4; greenish with brown markings

Incubation: 32–36 days; female and male incubate

Fledging: 28–32 days; male and female feed the young

Migration: complete, to southern states and Mexico; non-migrator in parts of South Dakota

Food: small birds, mammals

Compare: Sharp-shinned Hawk (p. 263) is much smaller, lighter gray and has a squared tail. Look for the banded, rounded tail to help identify Cooper's Hawk.

Stan's Notes: Resident hawk in Dakota woodlands. Stubby wings help it to navigate around trees while it chases small birds. Will ambush prey, flying into heavy brush or even running on the ground. Comes to feeders, hunting for birds. Flies with long glides followed by a few quick flaps. Calls a loud, clear "cack-cack-cack-cack." The young have gray eyes that turn bright yellow at 1 year and turn dark red later, after 3–5 years.

juvenile

in-flight
juvenile

in flight

Peregrine Falcon
Falco peregrinus

Size: 16–20" (41–51 cm); up to 3¾' wingspan

Male: Dark-gray back and tan-to-white chest. Horizontal bars on belly, legs and undertail. Dark "hood" head marking and wide black mustache. Yellow base of bill and eye-ring. Yellow legs.

Female: similar to male but noticeably larger

Juvenile: overall darker than adults, with heavy streaking on the chest and belly

Nest: ground (scrape) on a cliff edge, tall building, bridge or smokestack; 1 brood per year

Eggs: 3–4; white, some with brown markings

Incubation: 29–32 days; female and male incubate

Fledging: 35–42 days; male and female feed the young

Migration: complete, to southern states

Food: birds (Rock Pigeons in cities; shorebirds and waterfowl in rural areas)

Compare: The American Kestrel (p. 161) is smaller and has 2 vertical black stripes on its face. Look for the dark "hood" head marking and mustache marks to identify the Peregrine Falcon.

Stan's Notes: A wide-bodied raptor that hunts many bird species. The larger females hunt larger prey. Lives in many cities, diving (stooping) on pigeons at speeds of up to 200 miles (322 km) per hour, which knocks them to the ground. Soars with its wings flat, often riding thermals. During courtship, the male brings food to the female and performs aerial displays. Likes to nest on a high ledge or platform for a good view of its territory. A solitary nester and monogamous.

female
p. 207

male

soaring

Northern Harrier
Circus hudsonius

YEAR-ROUND
SUMMER

Size: 18–22" (45–56 cm); up to 4' wingspan

Male: Slender, low-flying hawk. Silver-gray with a large white rump patch and white belly. Long tail with faint narrow bands. Black wing tips. Yellow eyes.

Female: dark-brown back, brown streaking on breast and belly, large white rump patch, thin black tail bands, black wing tips, yellow eyes

Juvenile: similar to female, with an orange breast

Nest: ground; female and male construct; 1 brood per year

Eggs: 4–8; bluish white without markings

Incubation: 31–32 days; female incubates

Fledging: 30–35 days; male and female feed the young

Migration: partial migrator, to southern states, Mexico and Central America; non-migrator in parts of South Dakota

Food: mice, snakes, insects, small birds

Compare: Slimmer than the Red-tailed Hawk (p. 211). Cooper's Hawk (p. 265) has a rusty breast. Look for a low-gliding hawk with a large white rump patch to identify the male Harrier.

Stan's Notes: One of the easiest of hawks to identify. Glides just above the ground, following the contours of the land while searching for prey. Holds its wings just above horizontal, tilting back and forth in the wind, similar to Turkey Vultures. Formerly called the Marsh Hawk due to its habit of hunting over marshes. Feeds and nests on the ground. Will also preen and rest on the ground. Unlike other hawks, mainly uses its hearing to find prey, followed by sight. At any age, has a distinctive owl-like face disk.

269

female
p. 199

male

Gadwall

Mareca strepera

SUMMER

Size: 19" (48 cm)

Male: A plump gray duck with a brown head and a distinctive black rump. White belly. Chestnut-tinged wings. Bright-white wing linings. Small white wing patch, seen when swimming. Gray bill.

Female: similar to female Mallard, a mottled brown with a pronounced color change from dark-brown body to light-brown neck and head, bright-white wing linings, small white wing patch, gray bill with orange sides

Juvenile: similar to female

Nest: ground; female lines the nest with fine grass and down feathers plucked from her chest; 1 brood per year

Eggs: 8–11; white without markings

Incubation: 24–27 days; female incubates

Fledging: 48–56 days; young feed themselves

Migration: complete, to southern states and Mexico

Food: aquatic insects

Compare: Male Gadwall is one of the few gray ducks. Look for its distinctive black rump.

Stan's Notes: A duck of shallow marshes. Consumes mostly plant material, dunking its head in water to feed rather than tipping forward, like other dabbling ducks. Walks well on land; feeds in fields and woodlands. Frequently in pairs with other duck species. Nests within 300 feet (90 m) of water. Establishes pair bond in winter.

in flight

Canada Goose
Branta canadensis

YEAR-ROUND
SUMMER

Size: 25–43" (64–109 cm); up to 5½' wingspan

Male: Large gray goose with a black neck and head. White chin and cheek strap.

Female: same as male

Juvenile: same as adults

Nest: platform, on the ground; female builds; 1 brood per year

Eggs: 5–10; white without markings

Incubation: 25–30 days; female incubates

Fledging: 42–55 days; male and female teach the young to feed

Migration: non-migrator to partial migrator, moves around to find open water

Food: aquatic plants, insects, seeds

Compare: Large goose that is rarely confused with any other bird.

Stan's Notes: Breeds throughout North and South Dakota. Flocks fly in a large V when traveling long distances. Begins breeding in the third year. Adults mate for many years. If threatened, they will hiss as a warning. Males stand as sentinels at the edge of their group and will bob their heads and become aggressive if approached. Adults molt their primary flight feathers while raising their young, rendering family groups temporarily flightless. Several subspecies vary in the U.S. Generally eastern groups are paler than western. Their size also varies, decreasing northward. The smallest subspecies is in the Arctic.

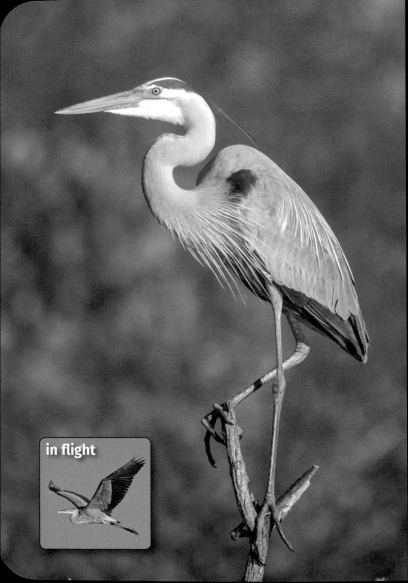

in flight

Great Blue Heron

Ardea herodias

SUMMER

Size: 42–48" (107–122 cm); up to 6' wingspan

Male: Tall and gray. Black eyebrows end in long plumes at the back of the head. Long yellow bill. Long feathers at the base of the neck drop down in a kind of necklace. Long legs.

Female: same as male

Juvenile: same as adults, but more brown than gray, with a black crown; lacks plumes

Nest: platform in a colony; male and female build; 1 brood per year

Eggs: 3–5; blue-green without markings

Incubation: 27–28 days; female and male incubate

Fledging: 56–60 days; male and female feed the young

Migration: complete, to southern states, Mexico, and Central and South America

Food: small fish, frogs, insects, snakes, baby birds

Compare: The Sandhill Crane (p. 277) has a red cap. Look for the long, yellow bill to help identify the Great Blue Heron.

Stan's Notes: One of the most common herons. Found in open water, from small ponds to large lakes. Stalks small fish in shallow water. Will strike at mice, squirrels and nearly anything it comes across. Red-winged Blackbirds will attack it to stop it from taking their babies out of the nest. In flight, it holds its neck in an S shape and slightly cups its wings, while the legs trail straight out behind. Nests in a colony of up to 100 birds. Nests in trees near or hanging over water. Barks like a dog when startled.

in flight

in-flight
rusty stain

rusty
stain

SUMMER MIGRATION

Sandhill Crane
Grus canadensis

Size: 42–48" (107–122 cm); up to 7' wingspan

Male: Elegant gray crane with long legs and neck. Wings and body often rust brown from mud staining. Scarlet-red cap. Yellow to red eyes.

Female: same as male

Juvenile: dull brown with yellow eyes; lacks a red cap

Nest: ground; female and male construct; 1 brood per year

Eggs: 2; olive with brown markings

Incubation: 28–32 days; female and male incubate

Fledging: 65 days; female and male feed the young

Migration: complete, to southern states and Mexico

Food: insects, fruit, worms, plants, amphibians

Compare: Great Blue Heron (p. 275) has a longer bill and holds its neck in an S shape during flight. Look for the scarlet-red cap to help identify the Sandhill Crane.

Stan's Notes: Preens mud into its feathers, staining its plumage rust brown (see insets). Gives a very loud and distinctive rattling call, often heard before the bird is seen. Flight is characteristic, with a faster upstroke, making the wings look like they're flicking in flight. Can fly at heights of over 10,000 feet (3,050 m). Nests on the ground in a large mound of aquatic vegetation. Performs a spectacular mating dance: The birds will face each other, then bow and jump into the air while making loud cackling sounds and flapping their wings. They will also flip sticks and grass into the air during their dance.

male

female

Ruby-throated Hummingbird

Archilochus colubris

SUMMER MIGRATION

Size: 3–3½" (7.5–9 cm)

Male: Tiny, iridescent green bird. Black throat patch reflects bright ruby red in direct sunlight.

Female: same as male but lacks a throat patch

Juvenile: same as female

Nest: cup; female builds; 1–2 broods per year

Eggs: 2; white without markings

Incubation: 12–14 days; female incubates

Fledging: 14–18 days; female feeds the young

Migration: complete, to southern states, Mexico and Central America

Food: nectar, insects; will come to nectar feeders

Compare: No other bird is as tiny. The Sphinx Moth also hovers at flowers, but it has clear wings, doesn't hum in flight, moves much slower than the Ruby-throated and can be approached.

Stan's Notes: This is the smallest bird in the Dakotas. Can fly straight up, straight down or backward and hover in midair. Does not sing but chatters or buzzes to communicate. Weighs about the same as a U.S. penny; it takes about five average-sized hummingbirds to equal the weight of one chickadee. The wings create the humming sound. Flaps 50–60 times or more per second when flying at top speed. Breathes 250 times per minute. Heart beats up to 1,260 times per minute. Builds a stretchy nest with plant material and spiderwebs, gluing pieces of lichen to the exterior for camouflage. Attracted to colorful, tubular flowers. Will extract and eat insects trapped in spiderwebs. A long-distance migrator, wintering as far south as the tropics of Central America.

male

female
p. 193

SUMMER
MIGRATION

Wood Duck

Aix sponsa

Size: 17–20" (43–51 cm)

Male: Small, highly ornamented dabbling duck. Mostly green head and crest patterned with black and white. Rusty chest and a white belly. Red eyes.

Female: brown duck with a bright-white eye-ring, not-so-obvious crest and blue patch on wings (speculum), often hidden

Juvenile: similar to female

Nest: cavity; female lines an old woodpecker cavity or a nest box in a tree; 1 brood per year

Eggs: 10–15; creamy white without markings

Incubation: 28–36 days; female incubates

Fledging: 56–68 days; female teaches the young to feed

Migration: complete, to southern states

Food: aquatic insects, plants, seeds

Compare: Male Northern Shoveler (p. 285) is larger with a long wide bill. Male Green-winged Teal (p. 183) lacks the Wood Duck's ornamental coloring.

Stan's Notes: A duck of quiet, shallow backwater ponds. Nearly extinct around 1900 due to overhunting, but doing well now. Nests in tree cavity or nest box. Seen flying in forests or perching on high branches. Female takes off with a loud squealing call and enters the nest cavity from full flight. Lays some eggs in a neighboring nest (egg dumping), resulting in more than 20 eggs in some clutches. Hatchlings stay in nest for 24 hours, then jump from as high as 60 feet (18 m) to the ground or water to follow their mother. They never return to the nest.

female
p. 203

male

Mallard
Anas platyrhynchos

YEAR-ROUND
SUMMER

Size: 19–21" (48–53 cm)

Male: Large, bulbous green head, white necklace and rust-brown or chestnut chest. Gray-and-white sides. Yellow bill. Orange legs and feet.

Female: brown with an orange-and-black bill and blue-and-white wing mark (speculum)

Juvenile: same as female but with a yellow bill

Nest: ground; female builds; 1 brood per year

Eggs: 7–10; greenish to whitish, unmarked

Incubation: 26–30 days; female incubates

Fledging: 42–52 days; female leads the young to food

Migration: non-migrator to partial in the Dakotas

Food: seeds, plants, aquatic insects; will come to ground feeders offering corn

Compare: Male Northern Shoveler (p. 285) has a white chest with rusty sides and a very large, spoon-shaped bill. Breeding male Northern Pintail (p. 205) has long tail feathers and a brown head. Look for the green head and yellow bill to identify the male Mallard.

Stan's Notes: A familiar dabbling duck of lakes and ponds. Also found in rivers, streams and some backyards. Tips forward to feed on vegetation on the bottom of shallow water. The name "Mallard" comes from the Latin word *masculus*, meaning "male," referring to the male's habit of taking no part in raising the young. Male and female have white underwings and white tails, but only the male has black central tail feathers that curl upward. Unlike the female, the male doesn't quack. Returns to its birthplace each year.

female
p. 201

male

Northern Shoveler

Spatula clypeata

SUMMER

Size: 19–21" (48–53 cm)

Male: Medium-sized duck with an iridescent green head, rust sides, white chest. Extraordinarily large, spoon-shaped bill, almost always held pointed toward the water.

Female: brown and black all over, green wing patch (speculum) and a large spoon-shaped bill

Juvenile: same as female

Nest: ground; female builds; 1 brood per year

Eggs: 9–12; olive without markings

Incubation: 22–25 days; female incubates

Fledging: 30–60 days; female leads the young to food

Migration: complete, to southern states, Mexico and Central America

Food: aquatic insects, plants

Compare: Male Mallard (p. 283) is similar, but it lacks the large spoon-shaped bill. The male Wood Duck (p. 281) is smaller and has a crest.

Stan's Notes: One of several species of shovelers. Called "Shoveler" due to the peculiar, shovel-like shape of its bill. Given the common name "Northern" because it is the only species of these ducks in North America. Seen in shallow wetlands, ponds and small lakes in flocks of 5–10 birds. Flocks fly in tight formation. Swims low in water, pointing its large bill toward the water as if it's too heavy to lift. Usually swims in tight circles while feeding. Feeds mainly by filtering tiny aquatic insects and plants from the surface of the water with its bill. Female gathers plant material and forms it into a nest a short distance from the water.

female
p. 321

male

SUMMER

American Redstart
Setophaga ruticilla

Size: 5" (13 cm)

Male: Striking black warbler with orange patches on the sides, wings and tail. White belly.

Female: olive-brown with yellow patches on the sides, wings and tail, white belly

Juvenile: same as female; male attains orange tinges in the second year

Nest: cup; female builds; 1 brood per year

Eggs: 3–5; off-white with brown markings

Incubation: 12 days; female incubates

Fledging: 9 days; female and male feed the young

Migration: complete, to Mexico, Central America and South America

Food: insects, seeds, occasionally berries

Compare: The male Baltimore Oriole (p. 289) and male Red-winged Blackbird (p. 31) are much larger. The male American Redstart is the only small black-and-orange bird flitting around the top of trees.

Stan's Notes: This is a common and widespread breeding warbler in the Dakotas. Found in woodlands, parks and yards and at forest edges. Prefers large, unbroken tracts of forest. Appears hyperactive when it feeds, hovering and darting back and forth to glean insects from leaves. Often droops wings and fans tail before launching out to catch an insect. Look for the flashing black-and-orange colors of the male high up in trees. First-year males have yellow markings and look like the females. Sings a high-pitched song that builds in intensity and then suddenly ends.

female
p. 331

male

Baltimore Oriole
Icterus galbula

SUMMER
MIGRATION

Size: 7–8" (18–20 cm)

Male: Flaming orange with a black head and back. White-and-orange wing bars. Orange-and-black tail. Gray bill and dark eyes.

Female: pale yellow with orange tones, gray-brown wings, white wing bars, gray bill, dark eyes

Juvenile: same as female

Nest: pendulous; female builds; 1 brood per year

Eggs: 4–5; bluish with brown markings

Incubation: 12–14 days; female incubates

Fledging: 12–14 days; female and male feed the young

Migration: complete, to Mexico, Central America and South America

Food: insects, fruit, nectar; comes to nectar, orange-half and grape-jelly feeders

Compare: The male American Redstart (p. 287) has much less orange. The male Orchard Oriole (p. 291) is much darker orange. Look for the flaming orange to identify the male Baltimore Oriole.

Stan's Notes: A fantastic songster, often heard before seen. Easily attracted to a feeder that offers sugar water (nectar), orange halves or grape jelly. Parents bring their young to feeders. Sits at the top of trees, feeding on caterpillars. Female builds a sock-like nest at the outermost branches of tall trees. Prefers parks, yards and forests and often returns to the same area year after year. Seen during migration and summer. Arrives in spring in May and June and some of the first to leave in the fall (August). Young males turn orange-and-black at 1½ years of age.

female
p. 333

male

first-year
male

Orchard Oriole
Icterus spurius

SUMMER

Size: 7–8" (18–20 cm)

Male: Dark orange with black head, throat, upper back, wings and tail. White wing bar. Bill is long and thin. Gray mark on lower bill.

Female: olive-green back, dull-yellow belly and gray wings with 2 indistinct white wing bars

Juvenile: same as female; first-year male looks like the female, with a black bib

Nest: pendulous; female builds; 1 brood per year

Eggs: 3–5; pale blue to white, brown markings

Incubation: 11–12 days; female and male incubate

Fledging: 11–14 days; female and male feed the young

Migration: complete, to central Mexico, Central America and northern South America

Food: insects, fruit, nectar; comes to nectar, orange-half and grape-jelly feeders

Compare: Similar to male Baltimore Oriole (p. 289), but it is a brighter orange. Look for the dark-orange plumage and all-black head to identify the Orchard Oriole.

Stan's Notes: Named "Orchard" for its preference for orchards. Also likes open woods. Eats insects until wild fruit starts to ripen. Often nests alone; sometimes nests in small colonies. Parents bring their young to bird feeding stations after they fledge. Many people don't see these birds at their feeders very much during the summer and think they have left, but the birds are still there, hunting for insects to feed to their young. One of the last birds to arrive in spring and one of the first to leave in fall.

male

female
p. 107

yellow
male

House Finch
Haemorhous mexicanus

YEAR-ROUND

Size: 5" (13 cm)

Male: Small finch with a red-to-orange face, throat, chest and rump. Brown cap. Brown marking behind eyes. White belly with brown streaks. Brown wings with white streaks.

Female: brown with a heavily streaked white chest

Juvenile: similar to female

Nest: cup, sometimes in cavities; female builds; 2 broods per year

Eggs: 4–5; pale blue, lightly marked

Incubation: 12–14 days; female incubates

Fledging: 15–19 days; female and male feed the young

Migration: non-migrator to partial migrator; moves around to find food

Food: seeds, fruit, leaf buds; visits seed feeders and feeders that offer grape jelly

Compare: Male Purple Finch (p. 295) is very similar, but male House Finch lacks the red crown. Look for the streaked breast and belly, and brown cap of male House Finch.

Stan's Notes: Can be common at feeders. A social bird, visits feeders in small flocks. Likes to nest in hanging flower baskets. Male sings a loud, cheerful warbling song. Historically it occurred from the Pacific to the Rockies, with only a few reaching the eastern side. Now found across the U.S. Suffers from a disease that causes the eyes to crust, resulting in blindness and death. Rarely, some males are yellow (see inset) instead of red, probably due to poor diet.

female
p. 123

male

Purple Finch
Haemorhous purpureus

MIGRATION
WINTER

Size:	6" (15 cm)
Male:	Raspberry-red head, cap, chest, back and rump. Brownish wings and tail. Large bill.
Female:	heavily streaked brown-and-white bird with bold white eyebrows
Juvenile:	same as female
Nest:	cup; female and male build; 1 brood per year
Eggs:	4–5; greenish blue with brown markings
Incubation:	12–13 days; female incubates
Fledging:	13–14 days; female and male feed the young
Migration:	irruptive; moves around in search of food
Food:	seeds, insects, fruit; comes to seed feeders
Compare:	The male House Finch (p. 293) has a brown cap and a streaked belly. Male Red Crossbill (p. 297) has a unique crossed bill. Look for the raspberry cap to help identify the male Purple Finch.

Stan's Notes: Usually only seen in the winter or during migration, when Purple Finches leave their northern homes and move around in search of food. Travels in flocks of up to 50 birds. Visits seed feeders along with House Finches, which makes it hard to tell them apart. Feeds mainly on seeds; ash tree seeds are an important source of food. Found in coniferous forests, mixed woods, woodland edges and suburban backyards. Flies in the typical undulating, up-and-down pattern of finches. Sings a rich, loud song. Gives a distinctive "tic" note only in flight. Male is not purple. The Latin species name *purpureus* means "purple" (or other reddish colors).

female
p. 327

male

Red Crossbill
Loxia curvirostra

YEAR-ROUND
SUMMER
MIGRATION
WINTER

Size: 6½" (16 cm)

Male: Sparrow-sized bird, dirty-red to orange with bright-red crown and rump. Long, pointed, crossed bill. Dark-brown wings and a short dark-brown tail.

Female: pale-yellow chest, light-gray throat patch, a crossed bill, dark-brown wings and tail

Juvenile: streaked with tinges of yellow, bill gradually crosses about 2 weeks after fledging

Nest: cup; female builds; 1 brood per year

Eggs: 3–4; bluish white with brown markings

Incubation: 14–18 days; female incubates

Fledging: 16–20 days; female and male feed young

Migration: non-migrator to irruptive; moves around the Dakotas in winter to find food

Food: seeds, leaf buds; comes to seed feeders

Compare: Similar in shape, size and color to the male Purple Finch (p. 295). Look for the male Red Crossbill's unique bill.

Stan's Notes: The long crossed bill is adapted for extracting seeds from pine and spruce cones, its favorite food. Often dangles upside down like a parrot to reach cones. Also seen on the ground where it eats grit, which helps digest food. Nests in coniferous forests. Plumage can be highly variable among individuals. While it is a resident nester in parts of the Dakotas, migrating crossbills from farther north move into North and South Dakota during winter, searching for food, swelling populations. This irruptive behavior makes it more common in some winters and nonexistent in others.

female
p. 151

male

juvenile

Northern Cardinal
Cardinalis cardinalis

YEAR-ROUND

Size: 8–9" (20–23 cm)

Male: Red with a black mask that extends from the face to the throat. Large crest and a large red bill.

Female: buff-brown with a black mask, large reddish bill, and red tinges on the crest and wings

Juvenile: same as female but with a blackish-gray bill

Nest: cup; female builds; 2–3 broods per year

Eggs: 3–4; bluish white with brown markings

Incubation: 12–13 days; female and male incubate

Fledging: 9–10 days; female and male feed the young

Migration: non-migrator

Food: seeds, insects, fruit; comes to seed feeders

Compare: Male Red Crossbill (p. 297) has dark brown wings and a thinner crossed bill. Look for the black mask, large crest and red bill to identify the male Northern Cardinal.

Stan's Notes: A familiar backyard bird. Seen in a variety of habitats, including parks. Usually likes thick vegetation. One of the few species in which both males and females sing. Can be heard all year. Listen for its "whata-cheer-cheer-cheer" territorial call in spring. Watch for a male feeding a female during courtship. The male also feeds the young of the first brood while the female builds a second nest. Territorial in spring, fighting its own reflection in a window or other reflective surface. Non-territorial in winter, gathering in small flocks of up to 20 birds. *Cardinalis* denotes importance, as represented by the red priestly garments of Catholic cardinals.

winter

breeding

SUMMER MIGRATION

Horned Grebe
Podiceps auritus

Size: 14" (36 cm)

Male: Breeding plumage (April to August) overall reddish with a black head. Rufous red neck and sides. Dark back. Yellow patch behind red eyes. Small black bill. Winter plumage has a black crown and white face, chin and neck. Red eyes and a white-tipped gray bill.

Female: same as male

Juvenile: similar to winter adult

Nest: floating platform, made of reeds and grass; female and male build; 1 brood per year

Eggs: 3–5; light blue with light markings

Incubation: 22–25 days; female and male incubate

Fledging: 20–40 days; male and female teach young what to eat

Migration: complete migrator, to the Pacific, Gulf and Atlantic coasts

Food: fish, aquatic insects

Compare: Eared Grebe (p. 39) is slightly smaller and has a black neck during breeding season.

Stan's Notes: A grebe of pothole lakes and ponds. Will often dive underwater to avoid danger, swimming up to 500 feet (150 m) before resurfacing. In an elaborate courtship display similar to the Western Grebe, male and female rise up side by side out of water and "rush" across the surface. Will shake heads and present weeds to each other as presents. Usually in pairs, building a platform nest in shallow water, continuing construction while female lays eggs. Young hatch several days apart. Chicks ride on backs of parents.

in flight

Forster's Tern
Sterna forsteri

Size: 14–15" (36–38 cm); up to 2½' wingspan

Male: White-and-gray tern with a jet-black crown. Leading edge of wings is gray, and trailing edge is white. Characteristic forked tail is long and white. Orange bill with a black tip. Winter plumage lacks the black crown, and the bill becomes nearly entirely black.

Female: same as male

Juvenile: similar to adults but lacks the black crown

Nest: floating platform; female and male build; 1 brood per year

Eggs: 3–5; tan to white with brown markings

Incubation: 23–24 days; female and male incubate

Fledging: 24–26 days; male and female feed the young

Migration: complete, to southern coastal states, Mexico and Central America

Food: small fish, insects

Compare: Similar to other terns. Look for the black crown and black-tipped orange bill of the breeding Forster's Tern.

Stan's Notes: Usually is seen in small colonies summering in the eastern Dakotas. Catches small fish by diving into water headfirst. Will catch insects in flight. Constructs a platform nest on floating vegetation. Nests in small colonies in shallow-water marshes. Was named after Johann Reinhold Forster, a German naturalist who traveled with Captain Cook in 1772.

in flight

breeding

juvenile

winter

Ring-billed Gull
Larus delawarensis

Size: 18–20" (45–51 cm); up to 4' wingspan

Male: White with gray wings, black wing tips spotted with white, and a white tail, seen in flight (inset). Yellow bill with a black ring near the tip. Yellowish legs and feet. In winter, the back of the head and the nape of the neck are speckled brown.

Female: same as male

Juvenile: white with brown speckles and a brown tip of tail; mostly dark bill

Nest: ground; female and male construct; 1 brood per year

Eggs: 2–4; off-white with brown markings

Incubation: 20–21 days; female and male incubate

Fledging: 20–40 days; female and male feed the young

Migration: complete, to southern states and Mexico

Food: insects, fish; scavenges for food

Compare: A large white-and-gray gull. Look for a black ring near the tip of a yellow bill, and yellow legs and feet.

Stan's Notes: A common gull of garbage dumps and parking lots. One of the most common gulls in the U.S. Hundreds of these birds often flock together. A three-year gull with different plumages in each of its first three years. Attains the ring on its bill after the first winter and adult plumage in the third year. Defends a small area around the nest, usually only a few feet.

in flight

Great Egret

Ardea alba

Size: 36–40" (91–102 cm); up to 4½' wingspan

Male: Tall, thin, all-white bird with a long neck and a long, pointed yellow bill. Black, stilt-like legs and black feet.

Female: same as male

Juvenile: same as adults

Nest: platform; male and female construct; 1 brood per year

Eggs: 2–3; light blue without markings

Incubation: 23–26 days; female and male incubate

Fledging: 43–49 days; female and male feed the young

Migration: complete, to southern states, Mexico and Central America

Food: small fish, aquatic insects, frogs, crayfish

Compare: Great Blue Heron (p. 275) is similar in shape, but it is larger and gray in color. Look for the long, thin white neck and long, pointed yellow bill to help identify the Great Egret.

Stan's Notes: A graceful, stately bird. Slowly stalks shallow ponds, lakes and wetlands in search of small fish to spear with its long, sharp bill. Holds neck in an S shape during flight. Nests in colonies with as many as 100 birds. Gives a loud, dry croak if disturbed or when squabbling for a nest site at the colony. The name "Egret" comes from the French word *aigrette,* meaning "ornamental tufts of plumes." The plumes grow near the tail during the breeding season. Hunted to near extinction in the 1800s and early 1900s for its beautiful long plumes, which were used to decorate hats for women. Today, the egret is a protected species.

blue morph

juvenile

white
morph

in flight

MIGRATION

Snow Goose
Chen caerulescens

Size: 25–38" (64–97 cm); up to 4½' wingspan

Male: White morph has black wing tips and varying patches of black and brown. Blue morph has a white head and a gray breast and back. Both morphs have a pink bill and legs.

Female: same as male

Juvenile: overall dull gray with a dark bill

Nest: ground; female builds; 1 brood per year

Eggs: 3–5; white without markings

Incubation: 23–25 days; female incubates

Fledging: 45–49 days; female and male teach the young to feed

Migration: complete, to, southern states, New Mexico, California and Mexico

Food: aquatic insects and plants

Compare: The Canada Goose (p. 273) is larger and has a black neck and white chin strap. Tundra and Trumpeter Swans (pp. 311 and 313, respectively) lack the black wing tips. The American White Pelican (p. 315) shares black wing tips, but it has an enormous bill.

Stan's Notes: This bird occurs in light (white) and dark (blue) color morphs. The white morph is more common than the blue. A bird of wide-open fields, wetlands and lakes of any size. It has a thick, serrated bill, which helps it to grab and pull up plants. Breeds in large colonies on the northern tundra in Canada. Female starts to breed at 2–3 years. Older females produce more eggs and are more successful at reproduction than younger females. Seen by the thousands during migration and in winter. Has a classic goose-like call.

juvenile

in flight

MIGRATION

Tundra Swan
Cygnus columbianus

Size: 50–54" (127–137 cm); up to 5½' wingspan

Male: Large all-white swan. Black bill, legs and feet. Small yellow mark in front of each eye.

Female: same as male

Juvenile: same size as adult with gray plumage, pinkish-gray bill

Nest: ground; female and male construct; 1 brood per year

Eggs: 4–5; creamy white without markings

Incubation: 35–40 days; female and male incubate

Fledging: 60–70 days; female and male feed the young

Migration: complete, to the East Coast

Food: plants, aquatic insects

Compare: The Trumpeter Swan (p. 313) is larger and lacks yellow marks on its face. Snow Goose (p. 309) is much smaller and has black wing tips. Look for the black bill and legs.

Stan's Notes: Nests on the tundra of northern Canada and Alaska, hence its common name. Migrates diagonally across North America to reach wintering grounds on the East Coast. Flies in large V-shaped wedges. Gathers in large numbers of several thousand during the winter. Often seen in large family groups of 20 or more individuals. Gives a high-pitched, whistle-like call. Young are easy to distinguish by their gray plumage and pinkish bills.

in flight

juvenile

SUMMER
MIGRATION

Trumpeter Swan
Cygnus buccinator

Size: 58–62" (147–157 cm); up to 6½' wingspan

Male: A large all-white swan with an all-black bill, legs and feet.

Female: same as male

Juvenile: same size as adult, with gray plumage and a pinkish-gray bill

Nest: ground; female and male construct; 1 brood per year

Eggs: 4–6; cream-white without markings

Incubation: 33–37 days; female incubates

Fledging: 100–120 days; female and male show the young what to eat

Migration: partial migrator to complete, to southern states; some will stay during winter on open water

Food: aquatic plants, insects

Compare: The Tundra Swan (p. 311) is very similar, but it has small yellow marks in front of its eyes (lores). Snow Goose (p. 309) is much smaller and has black wing tips.

Stan's Notes: Was once eliminated from both states due to market hunting, but reintroduced with great success. Reintroduced birds are identified by large colored tags on the neck or wings. Most breeding programs were started with eggs taken from Trumpeters in Alaska. Often on larger rivers. Also in wetlands, marshes, small lakes, ponds and farm fields. Mated pairs defend large territories and construct large mound nests at the edge of water. Many flock to open water on the Missouri River in winter. Named for its loud, trumpet-like call, typically given in flight.

breeding

in flight

chick-feeding
adult

American White Pelican
Pelecanus erythrorhynchos

SUMMER
MIGRATION

Size: 60–64" (152–163 cm); up to 9' wingspan

Male: Large white pelican with an enormous bright-yellow-to-orange bill. Yellow legs and feet. Black wing tips and trailing edge of wings. Breeding plumage has a bright-orange bill, legs and feet. Chick-feeding adult (an adult that is feeding young) has a gray-black crown.

Female: same as male

Juvenile: duller white than adult, with a brownish head and neck

Nest: ground, scraped-out depression rimmed with dirt; female and male build; 1 brood per year

Eggs: 1–3; white without markings

Incubation: 29–36 days; male and female incubate

Fledging: 60–70 days; female and male feed the young

Migration: complete, to Central and South America

Food: fish

Compare: Snow Goose (p. 309) is much smaller and lacks the Pelican's enormous bill. Look for the Pelican's black wing tips in flight.

Stan's Notes: Frequently seen in large groups on the larger lakes and reservoirs of the Dakotas during migration and summer. Doesn't dive to catch fish, like coastal Brown Pelicans (not shown). Instead, groups swim and dip their bills simultaneously into water to scoop up fish. Groups fly in a large V, often gliding, followed by simultaneous flapping. Large flocks swirl on columns of rising warm air (thermals) on hot days. Breeding adults typically grow a flat, fibrous plate on the upper bill, which drops off after the eggs hatch. Usually silent; gives short grunts at the nesting colony.

male

winter male

female

American Goldfinch
Spinus tristis

YEAR-ROUND
SUMMER

Size: 5" (13 cm)

Male: Canary-yellow finch with a black forehead and tail. Black wings with white wing bars. White rump. No markings on the chest. Winter male is similar to the female.

Female: dull olive-yellow plumage with brown wings; lacks a black forehead

Juvenile: same as female

Nest: cup; female builds; 1 brood per year

Eggs: 4–6; pale blue without markings

Incubation: 10–12 days; female incubates

Fledging: 11–17 days; female and male feed the young

Migration: partial migrator to non-migrator; small flocks of up to 20 birds move around to find food

Food: seeds, insects; will come to seed feeders

Compare: The Pine Siskin (p. 105) has a streaked chest and belly, with yellow wing bars. Female House Finch (p. 107) and female Purple Finch (p. 123) both have heavily streaked chests. Male Yellow Warbler (p. 323) is all yellow with orange streaks on chest.

Stan's Notes: A common backyard resident. Most often found in open fields, scrubby areas and woodlands. Enjoys Nyjer seed in feeders. Lines its nest with the silky down from wild thistle. Almost always in small flocks. Twitters while it flies. Flight is roller coaster-like. Often called Wild Canary due to the male's canary-colored plumage. Male sings a pleasant, high-pitched song. Moves only far enough south to find food.

male

female

Common Yellowthroat

Geothlypis trichas

SUMMER

Size: 5" (13 cm)

Male: Olive-brown with a bright-yellow throat and chest, a white belly and a distinctive black mask outlined in white. Long, thin, pointed black bill.

Female: similar to male but lacks a black mask

Juvenile: same as female

Nest: cup; female builds; 2 broods per year

Eggs: 3–5; white with brown markings

Incubation: 11–12 days; female incubates

Fledging: 10–11 days; female and male feed the young

Migration: complete, to southern states, Mexico and Central America

Food: insects

Compare: The male American Goldfinch (p. 317) has a black forehead and wings. Male Yellow Warbler (p. 323) has fine orange streaks on chest and lacks the black mask. The Yellow-rumped Warbler (p. 237) only has patches of yellow and lacks the yellow chest of the Yellowthroat.

Stan's Notes: A common warbler of open fields and marshes. Sings a cheerful, well-known "witchity-witchity-witchity-witchity" song from deep within tall grasses. Male sings from prominent perches and while he hunts. He performs a curious courtship display, bouncing in and out of tall grass while singing a mating song. Female builds a nest low to the ground. Young remain dependent on their parents longer than most other warblers. A frequent cowbird host.

American Redstart
Setophaga ruticilla

SUMMER

Size:	5" (13 cm)
Female:	Olive-brown warbler with yellow patches on the sides, wings and tail. White belly.
Male:	black with orange patches on the sides, wings and tail; white belly
Juvenile:	same as female; male attains orange tinges in the second year
Nest:	cup; female builds; 1 brood per year
Eggs:	3–5; off-white with brown markings
Incubation:	12 days; female incubates
Fledging:	9 days; female and male feed the young
Migration:	complete, to Mexico, Central America and South America
Food:	insects, seeds, occasionally berries
Compare:	The female Yellow-rumped Warbler (p. 237) is similar, but it has a yellow patch on its rump. Look for yellow patches on the sides, wings and tail to help identify the female Redstart.

Stan's Notes: This is a common and widespread breeding warbler in the Dakotas. Found in woodlands, parks and yards and at forest edges. Prefers large, unbroken tracts of forest. Appears hyperactive when it feeds, hovering and darting back and forth to glean insects from leaves. Often droops wings and fans tail before launching out to catch an insect. Look for the flashing black-and-orange colors of the male high up in trees. First-year males have yellow markings and look like the females. Sings a high-pitched song that builds in intensity and then suddenly ends.

male

female

Yellow Warbler
Setophaga petechia

Size: 5" (13 cm)

Male: Yellow with thin orange streaks on the chest and belly. Long, pointed dark bill.

Female: same as male but lacks orange streaks

Juvenile: similar to female but much duller

Nest: cup; female builds; 1 brood per year

Eggs: 4–5; white with brown markings

Incubation: 11–12 days; female incubates

Fledging: 10–12 days; female and male feed the young

Migration: complete, to southern states, Mexico, and Central and South America

Food: insects

Compare: Yellow-rumped Warbler (p. 237) has only spots of yellow, compared with the orange streaking on chest of male Yellow Warbler. The male American Goldfinch (p. 317) has a black forehead and black wings. Look for the orange streaks on the chest to identify the male Yellow Warbler. The female American Goldfinch (p. 317) has white wing bars.

Stan's Notes: A scattered but widespread breeding warbler in the Dakotas. More common in eastern areas, it is seen in gardens and shrubby areas close to water. A prolific insect eater, gleaning caterpillars and other insects from tree leaves. Male sings a string of notes that sound like "sweet, sweet, sweet, I'm-so-sweet!" Begins to migrate south in August. Returns in May and June. Males arrive in spring before females to claim territories. Migrates at night in mixed flocks of warblers. Rests and feeds during the day.

Dickcissel

Spiza americana

SUMMER

Size: 6" (15 cm)

Male: A small, thick-billed bird with yellow chest, belly and eyebrows. A distinctive black bib under a white chin. Chestnut wings.

Female: same as male, but lacking the black bib

Juvenile: similar to female, only duller overall

Nest: cup, made of plant stems, grass and leaves; female builds; 1 brood per year

Eggs: 4–6; pale blue without markings

Incubation: 12–13 days; female incubates

Fledging: 9–11 days; female feeds young

Migration: complete, to Mexico, Central America and South America

Food: insects, seeds

Compare: The western Meadowlark (p. 337) is larger and has a prominent black V-shaped necklace unlike the Dickcissel's black bib.

Stan's Notes: Originally a bird of the prairie, now found in alfalfa fields, abandoned fields and meadows due to the loss of native prairie habitat. Prefers habitat that is sparsely vegetative. Doesn't do well in thick, dense vegetation. The males arrive at breeding sites a couple weeks before the females and begin to sing from prominent perches. Often seen singing from a fence post because it's the tallest object around. Nest is bulky, only a couple feet above ground and usually well concealed. Common name comes from an imitation of its song.

male
p. 297

female

Red Crossbill
Loxia curvirostra

YEAR-ROUND
SUMMER
MIGRATION
WINTER

Size: 6½" (16 cm)

Female: A pale yellow-gray sparrow-sized bird with a pale-yellow chest and light-gray patch on the throat. Long, pointed, crossed bill. Dark-brown wings and a short dark-brown tail.

Male: dirty-red to orange with a bright-red crown and rump, a crossed bill, dark-brown wings and a short dark-brown tail

Juvenile: streaked with tinges of yellow, bill gradually crosses about 2 weeks after fledging

Nest: cup; female builds; 1 brood per year

Eggs: 3–4; bluish white with brown markings

Incubation: 14–18 days; female incubates

Fledging: 16–20 days; female and male feed young

Migration: non-migrator to irruptive; moves around the Dakotas in winter in search of food

Food: seeds, leaf buds; comes to seed feeders

Compare: Female Purple Finch (p. 123) is similar in size and shape. Look for the female Red Crossbill's unique bill.

Stan's Notes: The long crossed bill is adapted for extracting seeds from pine and spruce cones, its favorite food. Often dangles upside down like a parrot to reach cones. Also seen on the ground where it eats grit, which helps digest food. Nests in coniferous forests. Plumage can be highly variable among individuals. Red Crossbills from farther north migrate into the Dakotas during winter, searching for food, swelling populations. This irruptive behavior makes it more common in some winters and nonexistent in others.

male

non-breeding
male

female

Western Tanager
Piranga ludoviciana

SUMMER
MIGRATION

Size: 7¼" (18.5 cm)

Male: A canary-yellow bird with a red head. Black back, tail, wings. One white and one yellow wing bar. Non-breeding lacks the red head.

Female: duller than male, lacking the red head

Juvenile: similar to female

Nest: cup; female builds; 1 brood per year

Eggs: 3–5; light blue with brown markings

Incubation: 14–18 days; female incubates

Fledging: 16–20 days; female and male feed young

Migration: complete, to Mexico and Central America

Food: insects, fruit

Compare: The unique coloring makes the breeding male Tanager easy to identify. Male American Goldfinch (p. 317) male has a black forehead. Female Orchard Oriole (p. 333) lacks the female Tanager's single yellow wing bars.

Stan's Notes: Seen during migration in parts of the Dakotas, it summers in the Black Hills of South Dakota. The male is stunning in its breeding plumage. Feeds mainly on insects, such as bees, wasps, cicadas and grasshoppers, and to a lesser degree on fruit. The male feeds the female while she incubates. Female builds a cup nest in a horizontal fork of a coniferous tree, well away from the main trunk, 20–40 feet (6–12 m) aboveground. This is the farthest-nesting tanager species, reaching far up into the Northwest Territories of Canada. An early fall migrant, often seen migrating in late July (when non-breeding males lack red heads). Seen in many habitats during migration.

male
p. 289

female

Baltimore Oriole

Icterus galbula

SUMMER MIGRATION

Size: 7–8" (18–20 cm)

Female: Pale yellow with orange tones and gray-brown wings with white wing bars. Gray bill. Dark eyes.

Male: flaming orange with a black head and back, white-and-orange wing bars, an orange-and-black tail, a gray bill and dark eyes

Juvenile: same as female

Nest: pendulous; female builds; 1 brood per year

Eggs: 4–5; bluish with brown markings

Incubation: 12–14 days; female incubates

Fledging: 12–14 days; female and male feed the young

Migration: complete, to Mexico, Central America and South America

Food: insects, fruit, nectar; comes to nectar, orange-half and grape-jelly feeders

Compare: The female Orchard Oriole (p. 333) has a dull-yellow belly. Look for the gray-brown wings to identify the female Baltimore Oriole.

Stan's Notes: A fantastic songster, often heard before seen. Easily attracted to bird feeders that offer sugar water (nectar), orange halves or grape jelly. Parents bring young to feeders. Sits at the top of trees, feeding on caterpillars. Female builds a sock-like nest at the outermost branches of tall trees. Prefers parks, yards and forests and often returns to the same area year after year. Seen during migration and summer. Arrives in spring in May and June and some of the first to leave in the fall (August). Young males turn orange-and-black at 1½ years of age.

male
p. 291

female

first-year
male

SUMMER

Orchard Oriole
Icterus spurius

Size: 7–8" (18–20 cm)

Female: Olive-green with a dull-yellow belly. Gray wings with 2 indistinct white wing bars. Long, thin bill with a gray mark on the lower bill.

Male: dark orange with black head, throat, upper back, wings and tail; 1 white wing bar

Juvenile: same as female; first-year male looks like the female, with a black bib

Nest: pendulous; female builds; 1 brood per year

Eggs: 3–5; pale blue to white, brown markings

Incubation: 11–12 days; female and male incubate

Fledging: 11–14 days; female and male feed the young

Migration: complete, to central Mexico, Central America and northern South America

Food: insects, fruit, nectar; comes to nectar, orange-half and grape-jelly feeders

Compare: Female Baltimore Oriole (p. 331) is similar, but it has orange tones and more pronounced wing bars.

Stan's Notes: Named "Orchard" for its preference for orchards. Also likes open woods. Eats insects until wild fruit starts to ripen. One of the last birds to arrive in spring and one of the first to leave in fall. Often nests alone; sometimes nests in small colonies. Parents bring their young to bird feeding stations after they fledge. Many people don't see these birds at feeders much during the summer and think they have left, but the birds are still there, hunting for insects to feed to their young.

Western Kingbird
Tyrannus verticalis

SUMMER

Size: 9" (22.5 cm)

Male: Bright-yellow belly and yellow under wings. Gray head and chest, often with white chin. Wings and tail are dark gray to nearly black with white outer edges on tail.

Female: same as male

Juvenile: similar to adult, less yellow and more gray

Nest: cup; female and male construct; 1 brood per year

Eggs: 3–4; white with brown markings

Incubation: 18–20 days; female incubates

Fledging: 16–18 days; female and male feed young

Migration: complete, to Central America

Food: insects, berries

Compare: The Eastern Kingbird (p. 243) lacks any yellow of the Western Kingbird. Western Meadowlark (p. 335) also shares the yellow belly of Western Kingbird, but it has a distinctive black V-shaped necklace.

Stan's Notes: A bird of open country, frequently seen sitting on top of the same shrub or fence post. Hunts by watching for crickets, bees, grasshoppers and other insects and flying out to catch them, then returns to perch. Parents teach young how to hunt, bringing wounded insects back to the nest for the young to chase. Returns in May. Builds nest in late May, often in a fork of a small single-trunk tree. More common in the western and central Dakotas, where it nests in trees around homesteads and farms.

Eastern
Meadowlark

Western Meadowlark
Sturnella neglecta

Size: 9" (22.5 cm)

Male: Heavy-bodied bird with a short tail. Yellow chest and brown back. Prominent V-shaped black necklace. White outer tail feathers.

Female: same as male

Juvenile: same as adult

Nest: cup, on the ground in dense cover; female builds; 2 broods per year

Eggs: 3–5; white with brown markings

Incubation: 13–15 days; female incubates

Fledging: 11–13 days; female and male feed young

Migration: non-migrator to partial migrator

Food: insects, seeds

Compare: Western Kingbird (p. 335) shares the yellow belly, but it lacks the V-shaped black necklace. Horned Lark (p. 141) lacks the yellow chest and belly. Look for a black V marking on the chest to help identify the Meadowlark.

Stan's Notes: Named "Meadowlark" because it's a bird of meadows and sings like the larks of Europe. Best known for its wonderful song—a flute-like, clear whistle. Not in the lark family; a blackbird family member and is related to grackles and orioles. Like other members of the blackbird family, the meadowlark catches prey by poking its long thin bill in places such as holes in the ground or tufts of grass, where insects are hiding. Overall population is down greatly due to agricultural activities and ditch mowing. Seen in the western two-thirds of the Dakotas, while Eastern Meadowlarks (see inset) occur in eastern areas (map reflects their combined range). Nearly identical in appearance, but they sing distinctly different songs.

BIRDING ON THE INTERNET

Birding online is a great way to discover additional information and learn more about birds. These websites will assist you in your pursuit of birds. Web addresses sometimes change a bit, so if one no longer works, just enter the name of the group into a search engine to track down the new address.

Site	Address
Author Stan Tekiela's homepage	naturesmart.com
Audubon Dakota Society	dakota.audubon.org
American Birding Association	aba.org
Black Hills Raptor Center	blackhillsraptorcenter.org
The Cornell Lab of Ornithology	birds.cornell.edu
eBird	ebird.org
North Dakota Birding Society	ndbirdingsociety.com
South Dakota Ornithologists' Union	sdou.org

CHECKLIST/INDEX BY SPECIES

Use the boxes to check the birds you've seen.

☐ Avocet, American 69

☐ Bittern, American 217

☐ Blackbird,
Red-winged 31, 153

☐ Blackbird,
Yellow-headed 35, 163

☐ Bluebird, Eastern 89

☐ Bluebird, Mountain 91

☐ Bunting, Lark 53, 129

☐ Bunting, Lazuli. 85, 115

☐ Bunting, Snow. 55

☐ Cardinal, Northern . . . 151, 299

☐ Catbird, Gray. 245

☐ Chickadee,
Black-capped 231

☐ Chicken, Greater Prairie-. . . 191

☐ Collared-Dove, Eurasian . . . 255

☐ Coot, American 41

☐ Cormorant,
Double-crested 47

☐ Cowbird,
Brown-headed 25, 143

☐ Crane, Sandhill 277

☐ Crossbill, Red 297, 327

☐ Crow, American 43

☐ Dickcissel 325

☐ Dove, Eurasian Collared-. . . 255

☐ Dove, Mourning 173

☐ Duck, Ring-necked 67, 189

☐ Duck, Wood 193, 281

☐ Eagle, Bald. 81

☐ Eagle, Golden 223

☐ Egret, Great 307

☐ Falcon, Peregrine 267

☐ Finch, House. 107, 293

☐ Finch, Purple. 123, 295

☐ Flicker, Northern 171

☐ Flycatcher, Great Crested. . . 241

☐ Gadwall 199, 271

☐ Goldeneye, Common . . . 71, 197

☐ Goldfinch, American 317

☐ Goose, Canada 273

☐ Goose, Greater
White-fronted 219

☐ Goose, Snow. 309

☐ Grackle, Common 37

☐ Grebe, Eared. 39

☐ Grebe, Horned. 301

☐ Grebe, Pied-billed. 177

☐ Grebe, Western 79

☐ Grosbeak,
Rose-breasted. 57, 139

☐ Gull, Franklin's 259

☐ Gull, Ring-billed. 305

☐ Harrier, Northern 207, 269

☐ Hawk, Cooper's 265

☐ Hawk, Ferruginous 215

☐ Hawk, Red-tailed 211

☐ Hawk, Sharp-shinned 263

☐ Hawk, Swainson's. 209

☐ Heron,
Black-crowned Night- 77

☐ Heron, Great Blue. 275

☐ Hummingbird,
Ruby-throated. 279

☐ Jay, Blue 95

☐ Junco, Dark-eyed 113, 233

☐ Kestrel, American 161

☐ Killdeer. 167

☐ Kingbird, Eastern 243

☐ Kingbird, Western 335

☐ Kingfisher, Belted 97

☐ Kinglet, Ruby-crowned 227

☐ Lark, Horned. 141

☐ Longspur,
Chestnut-collared. 125

☐ Longspur, Lapland 127

☐ Magpie, Black-billed 73

☐ Mallard. 203, 283

☐ Martin, Purple. 93

☐ Meadowlark, Eastern 337

☐ Meadowlark, Western. 337

☐ Nighthawk, Common 157

☐ Night-Heron,
Black-crowned 77

☐ Nuthatch, Red-breasted . . .229

☐ Nuthatch,
White-breasted 235

☐ Oriole, Baltimore 289, 331

☐ Oriole, Orchard 291, 333

☐ Osprey 75

☐ Owl, Burrowing 159

☐ Owl, Eastern Screech- 249

☐ Owl, Great Horned 213

☐ Pelican, American White . . . 315

☐ Phalarope, Wilson's. 251

☐ Pheasant, Ring-necked. . . . 221

☐ Phoebe, Eastern. 239

☐ Pigeon, Rock. 257

☐ Pintail, Northern 205

☐ Prairie-Chicken, Greater . . . 191

☐ Redpoll, Common. 101

☐ Redstart, American . . . 287, 321

☐ Robin, American 253

☐ Sandpiper, Spotted 149

☐ Sandpiper, Upland 175

☐ Scaup, Lesser 65, 187

☐ Screech-Owl, Eastern 249

☐ Shoveler, Northern . . . 201, 285

☐ Shrike, Loggerhead 247

☐ Siskin, Pine 105

☐ Sparrow, American Tree . . . 119

☐ Sparrow, Chipping 103

☐ Sparrow, Harris's 147

☐ Sparrow, House 121

☐ Sparrow, Lark 131

☐ Sparrow, Song 111

☐ Sparrow, White-crowned . . . 135

☐ Sparrow, White-throated . . . 133

☐ Starling, European 27

☐ Swallow, Barn 87

☐ Swallow, Cliff 117

☐ Swallow, Tree 83

☐ Swan, Trumpeter 313

☐ Swan, Tundra 311

☐ Swift, Chimney 99

☐ Tanager, Western 329

☐ Teal, Blue-winged 185

☐ Teal, Green-winged 183

☐ Tern, Black 33

☐ Tern, Forster's 303

☐ Thrasher, Brown 169

☐ Thrush, Swainson's 137

☐ Towhee, Spotted 29, 155

☐ Turkey, Wild 225

☐ Vulture, Turkey 45

☐ Warbler,
Black-and-white 49

☐ Warbler, Yellow 323

☐ Warbler, Yellow-rumped . . . 237

☐ Waxwing, Bohemian 145

☐ Waxwing, Cedar 145

☐ Wigeon, American 195

☐ Willet 181, 261

☐ Woodpecker, Downy 51

☐ Woodpecker, Hairy 59

☐ Woodpecker,
Red-bellied 63

☐ Woodpecker,
Red-headed 61

☐ Wren, House 109

☐ Yellowlegs, Greater 179

☐ Yellowlegs, Lesser 165

☐ Yellowthroat, Common 319

MORE FOR THE DAKOTAS BY STAN TEKIELA

Identification Guides
Birds of Prey of the Midwest
Field Guide
Birds of the Dakotas Field Guide

Nature Books
Bird Trivia
Stan Tekiela's Birding for
Beginners: Midwest
Start Mushrooming
A Year in Nature with Stan Tekiela

Children's Books:
Adventure Board Book Series
Floppers & Loppers
Paws & Claws
Peepers & Peekers
Snouts & Sniffers

Children's Books
C is for Cardinal
Can You Count the Critters?
Critter Litter

Children's Books:
Wildlife Picture Books
Baby Bear Discovers the World
The Cutest Critter
Do Beavers Need Blankets?
Hidden Critters
Jump, Little Wood Ducks
Some Babies Are Wild
Super Animal Powers
What Eats That?
Whose Baby Butt?
Whose Butt?
Whose House Is That?
Whose Track Is That?

Favorite Wildlife
Bald Eagles
Hummingbirds
Loons

Wildlife Appreciation Series
Backyard Birds
Bears
Bird Migration
Cranes, Herons & Egrets
Deer, Elk & Moose
Intriguing Owls
Wild Birds

Nature Appreciation Series
Bird Nests
Feathers
Wildflowers

Our Love of Wildlife Series
Our Love of Loons
Our Love of Owls

Adventure Quick Guides
Birds of the Prey of the Midwest
Birds of the Midwest
Wildflowers of the Midwest

Nature's Wild Cards (playing cards)
Bears
Birds of the Midwest
Hummingbirds
Loons
Mammals of the Midwest
Owls
Raptors
Trees of the Midwest
Wildflowers of the Midwest

ABOUT THE AUTHOR

Naturalist, wildlife photographer and writer Stan Tekiela is the originator of the popular state-specific field guide series that includes the *Birds of Minnesota Field Guide*. Stan has authored more than 190 educational books, including field guides, quick guides, nature books, children's books and more, presenting many species of animals and plants.

With a Bachelor of Science degree in natural history from the University of Minnesota and as an active professional naturalist for more than 30 years, Stan studies and photographs wildlife throughout the United States and Canada. He has received national and regional awards for his books and photographs and is also a well-known columnist and radio personality. His syndicated column appears in more than 25 newspapers, and his wildlife programs are broadcast on a number of Midwest radio stations. You can follow Stan on Facebook and Twitter or contact him via his website, naturesmart.com.

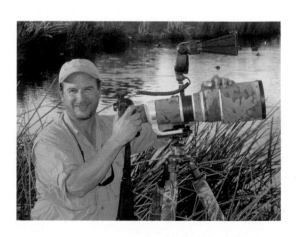